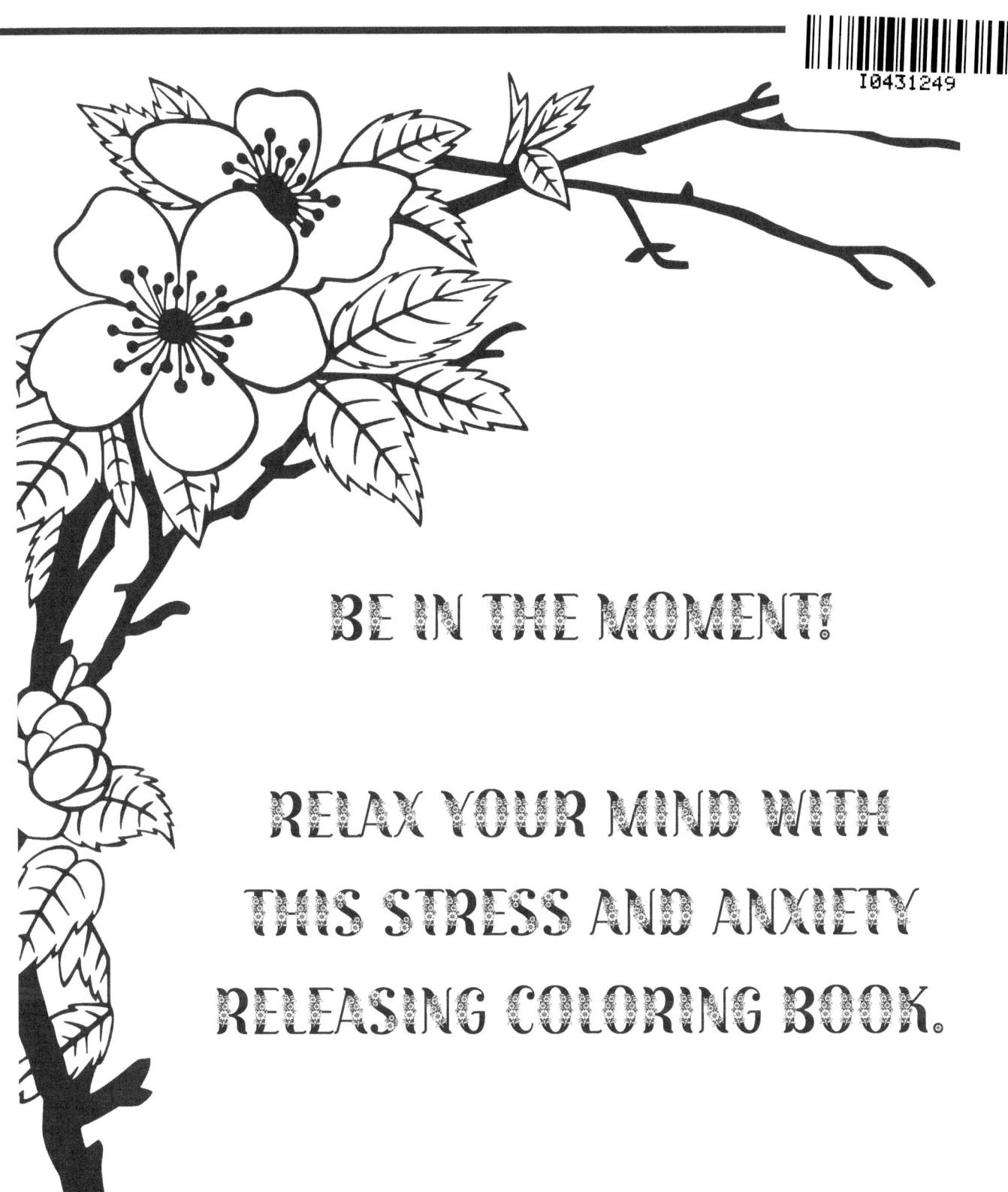

BE IN THE MOMENT!

RELAX YOUR MIND WITH THIS STRESS AND ANXIETY RELEASING COLORING BOOK.

Copyright © 2022 by Lady Sumone
All rights reserved. This book or any portion thereof
may not be reproduced or used in any manner whatsoever
without the express written permission of the publisher
except for the use of brief quotations in a book review.

This Book Belongs To:

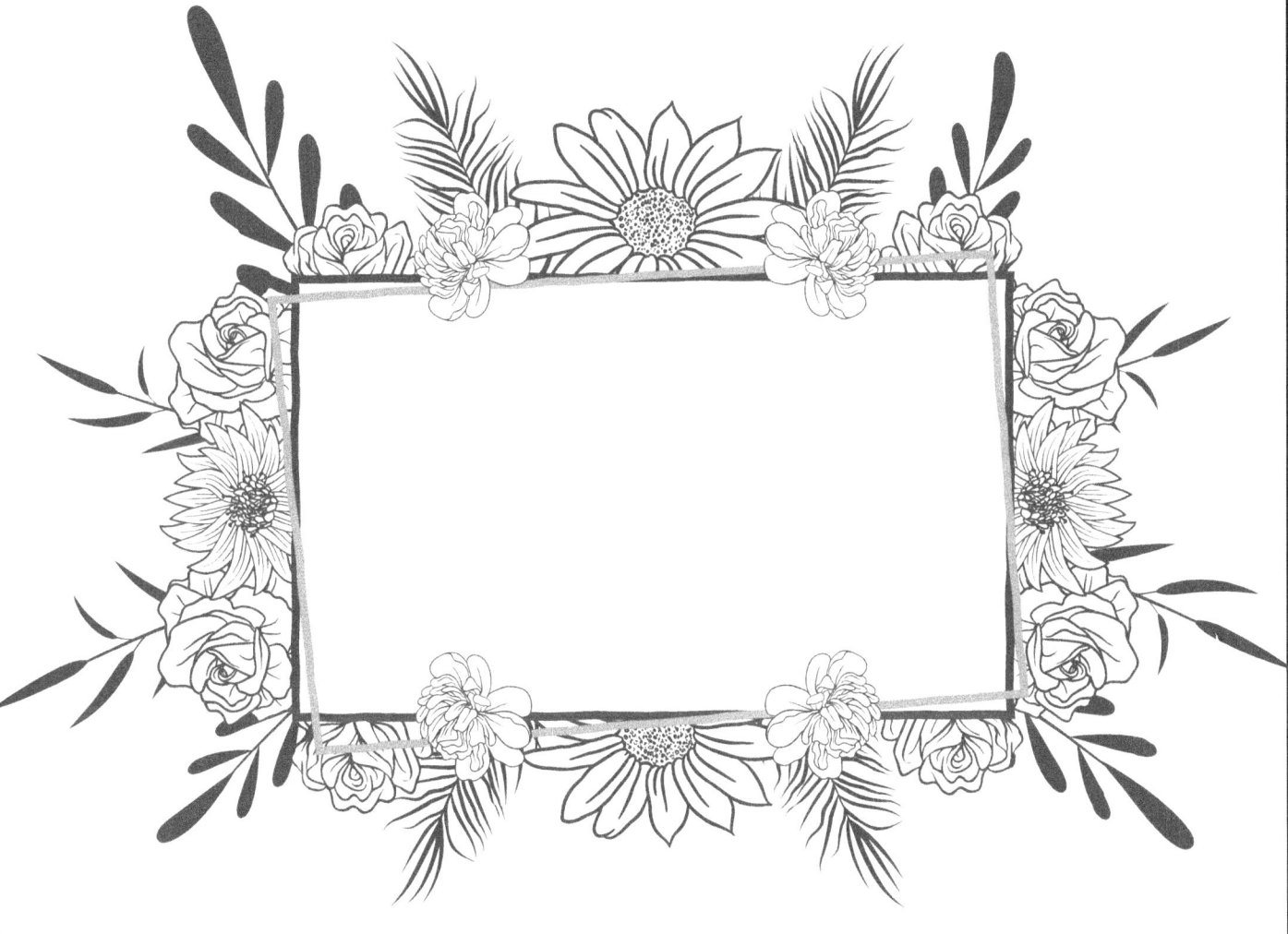

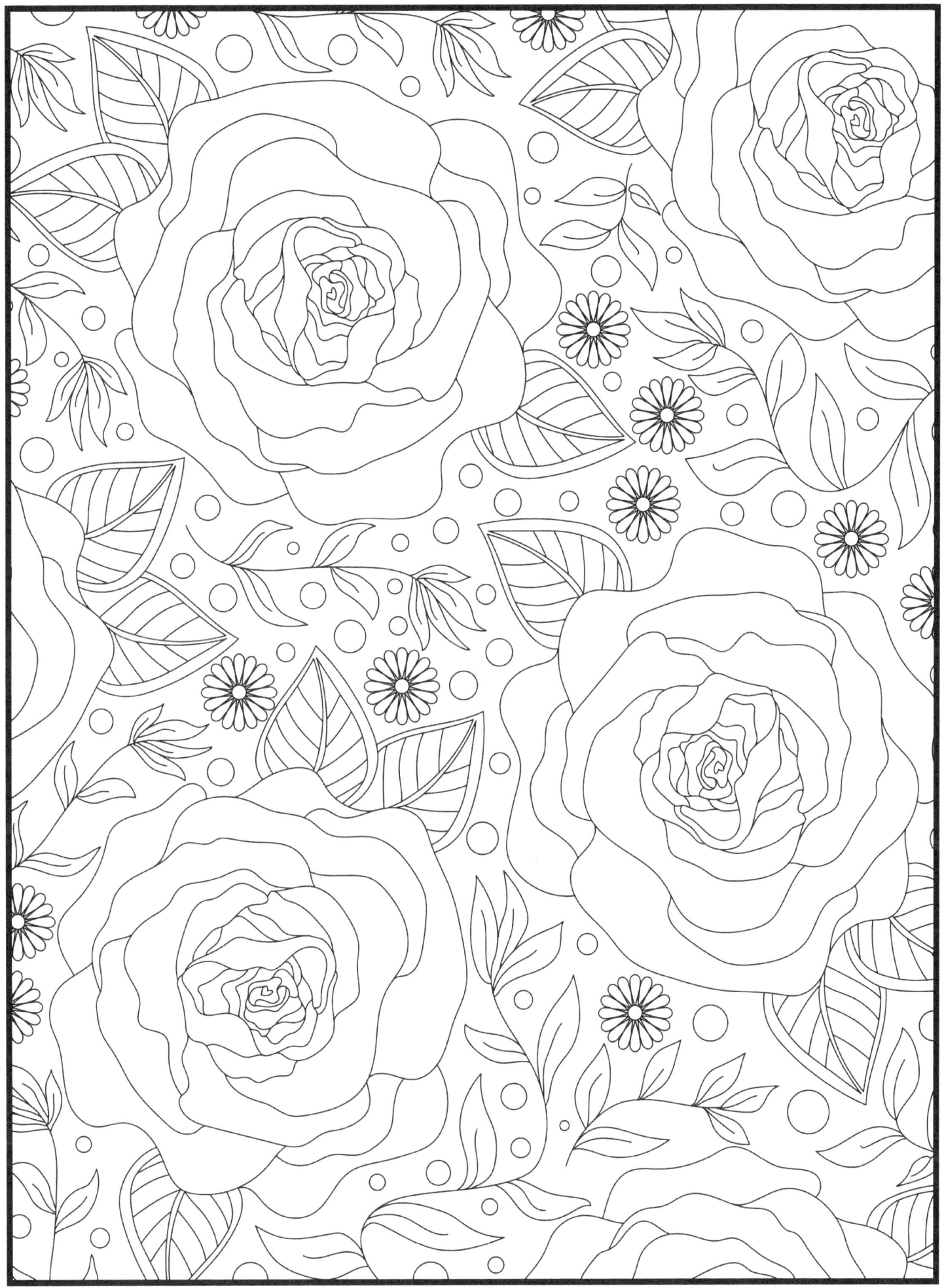

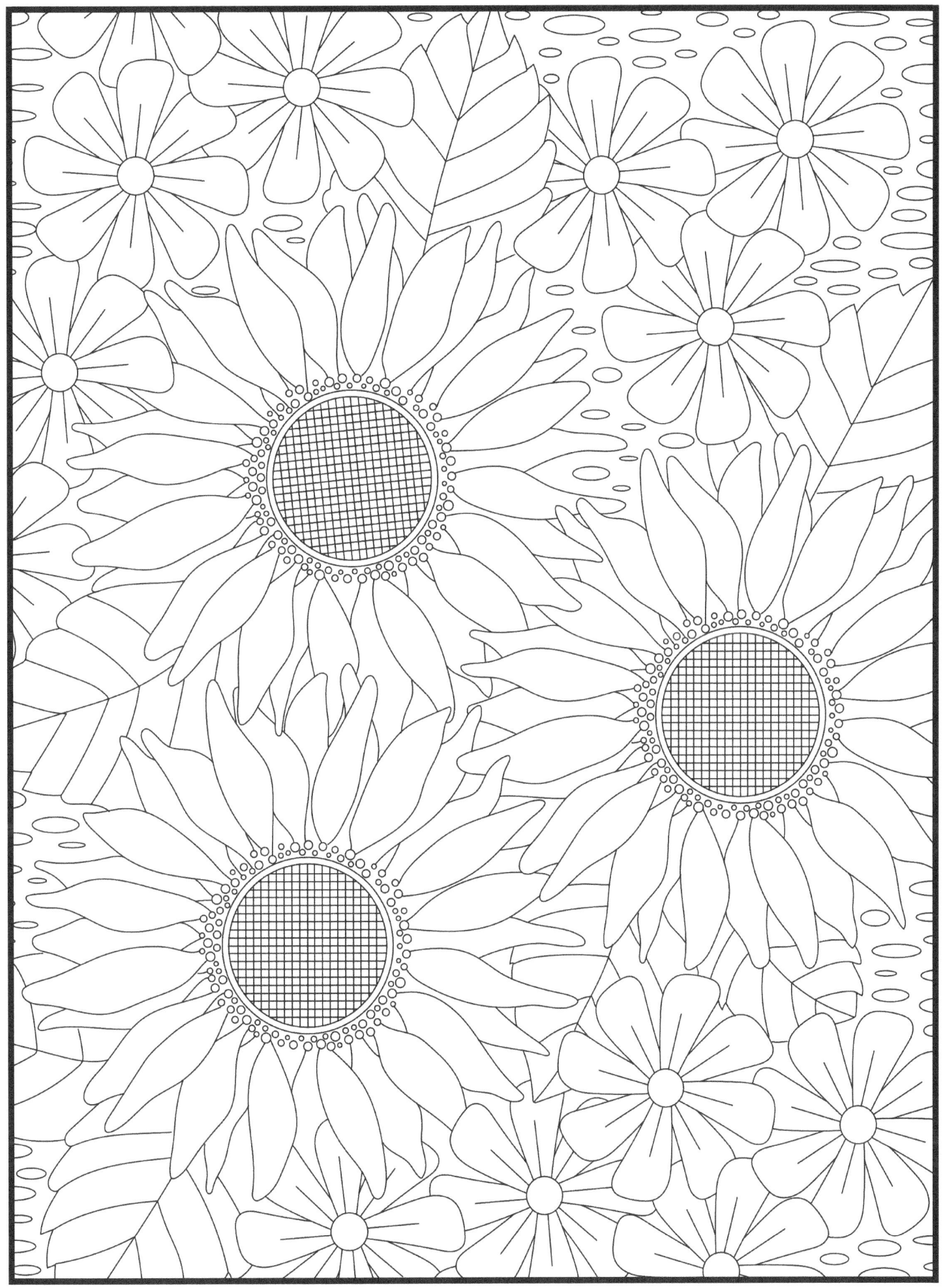

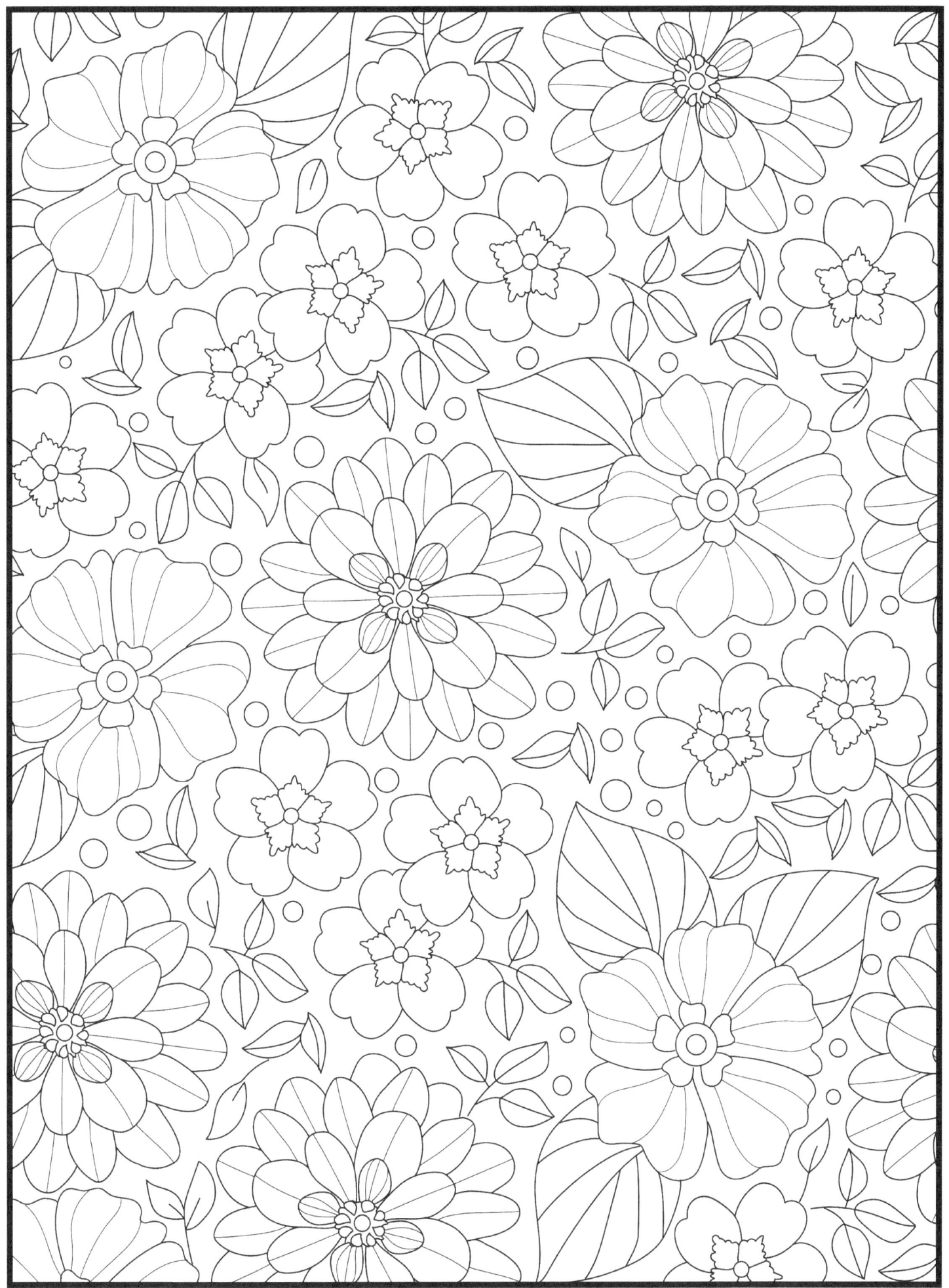

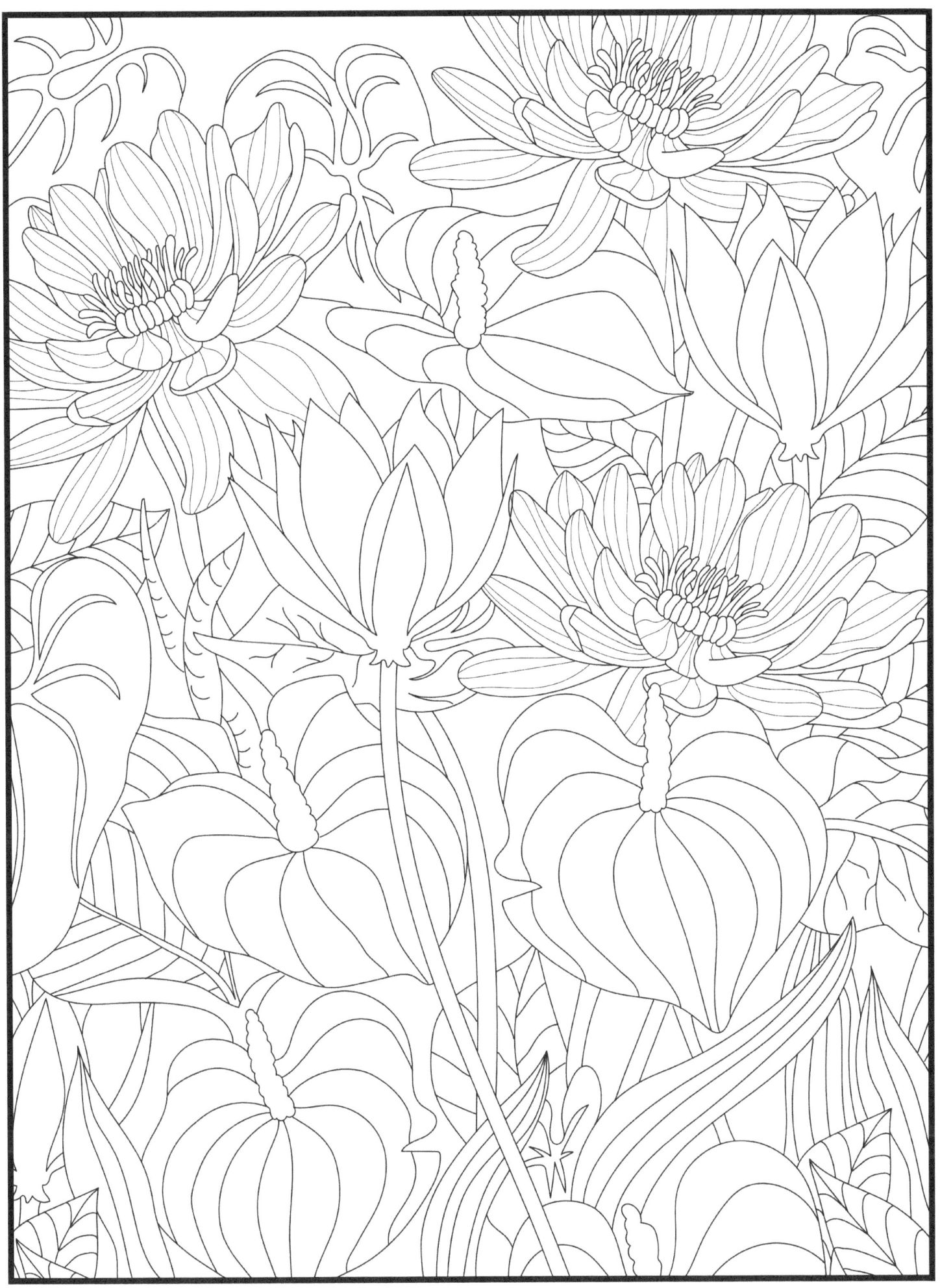

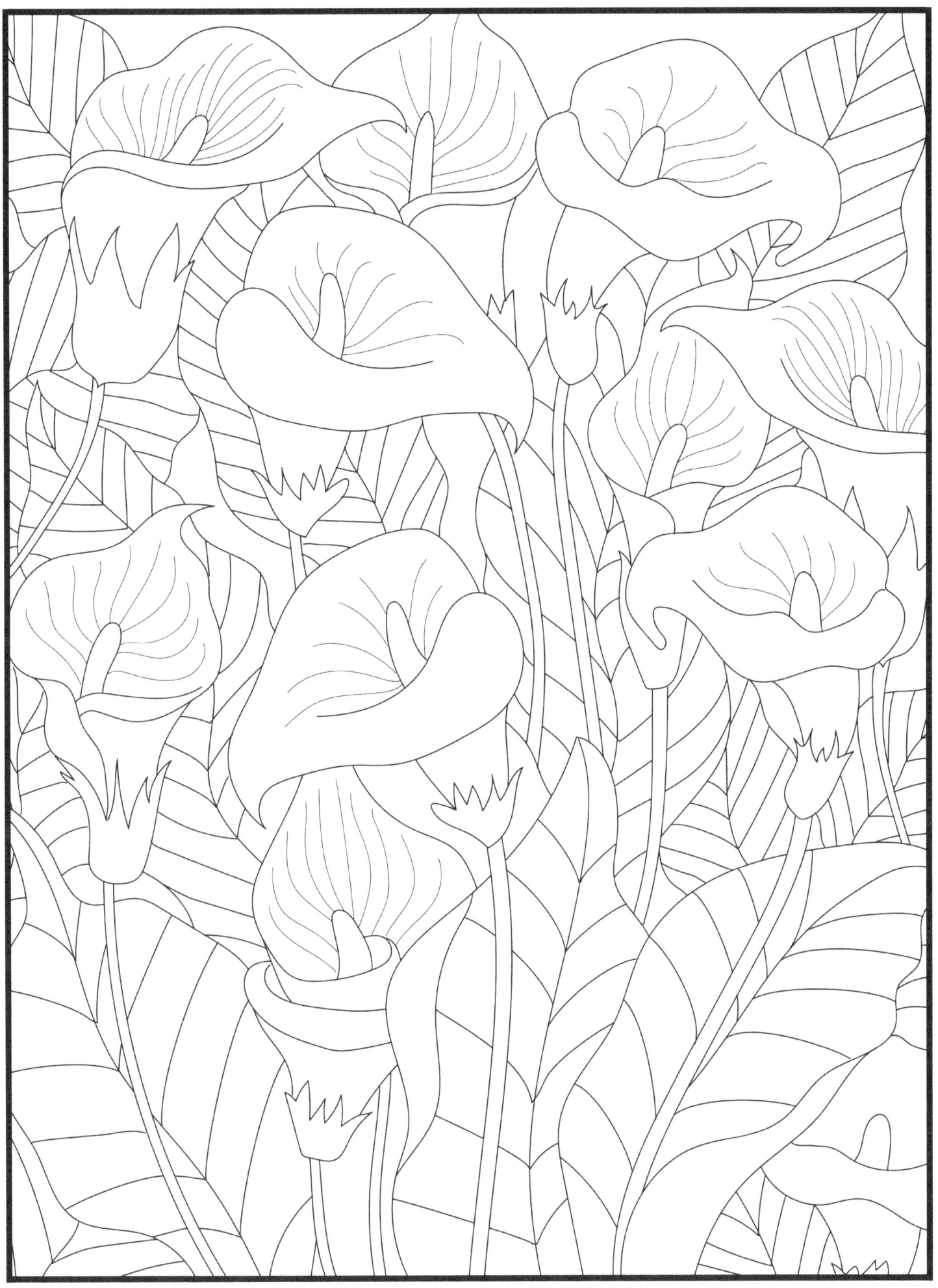

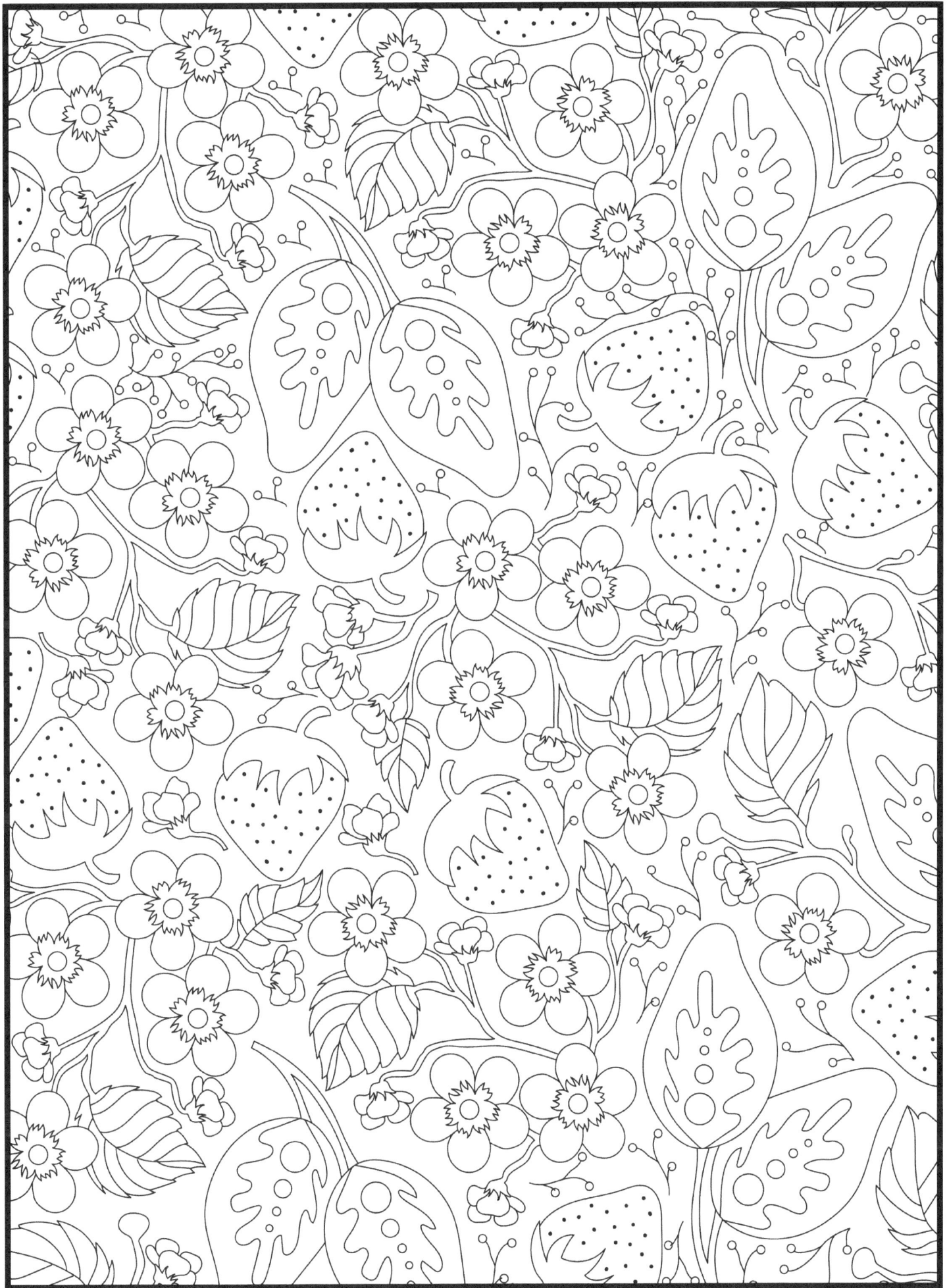

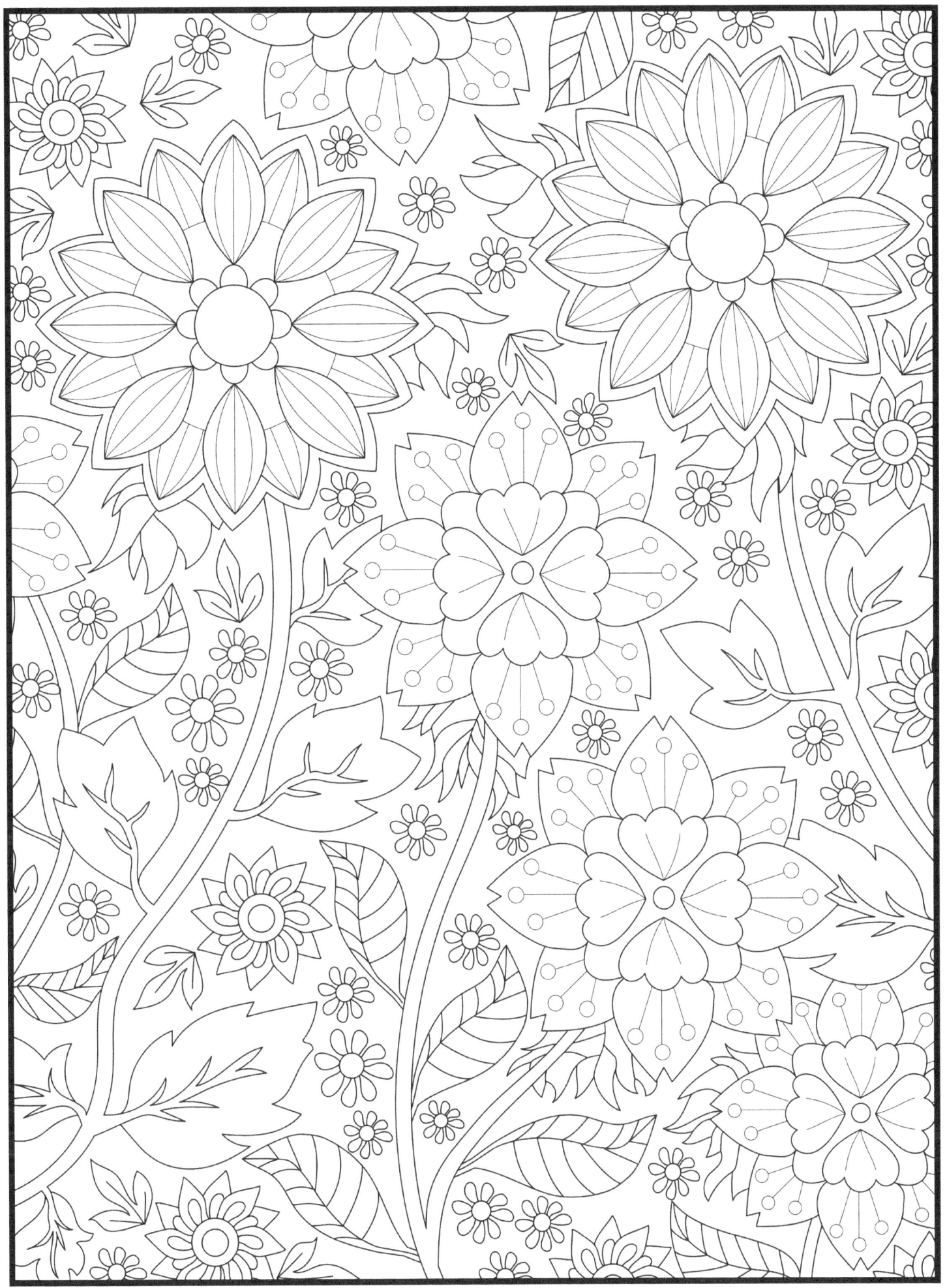

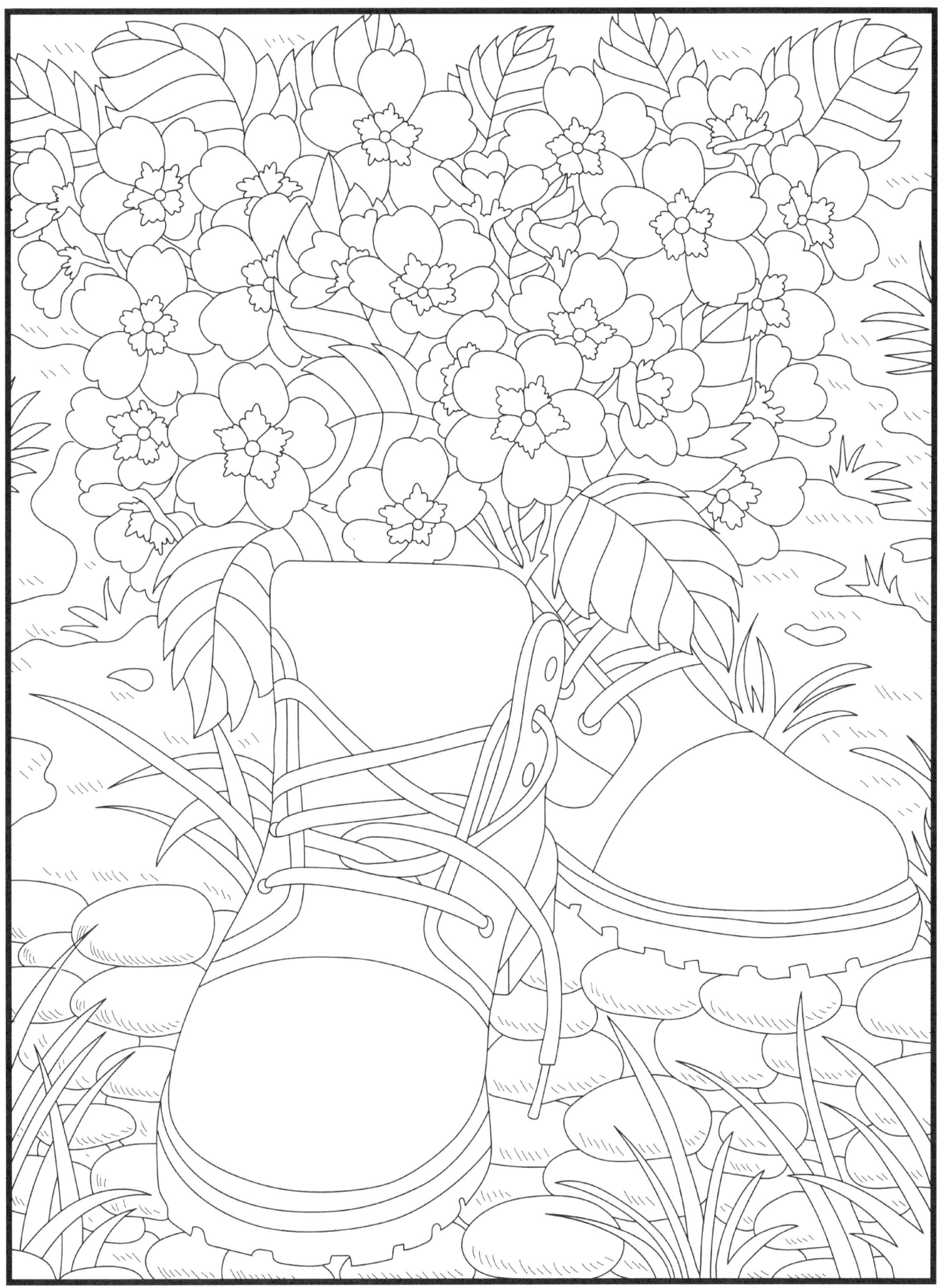

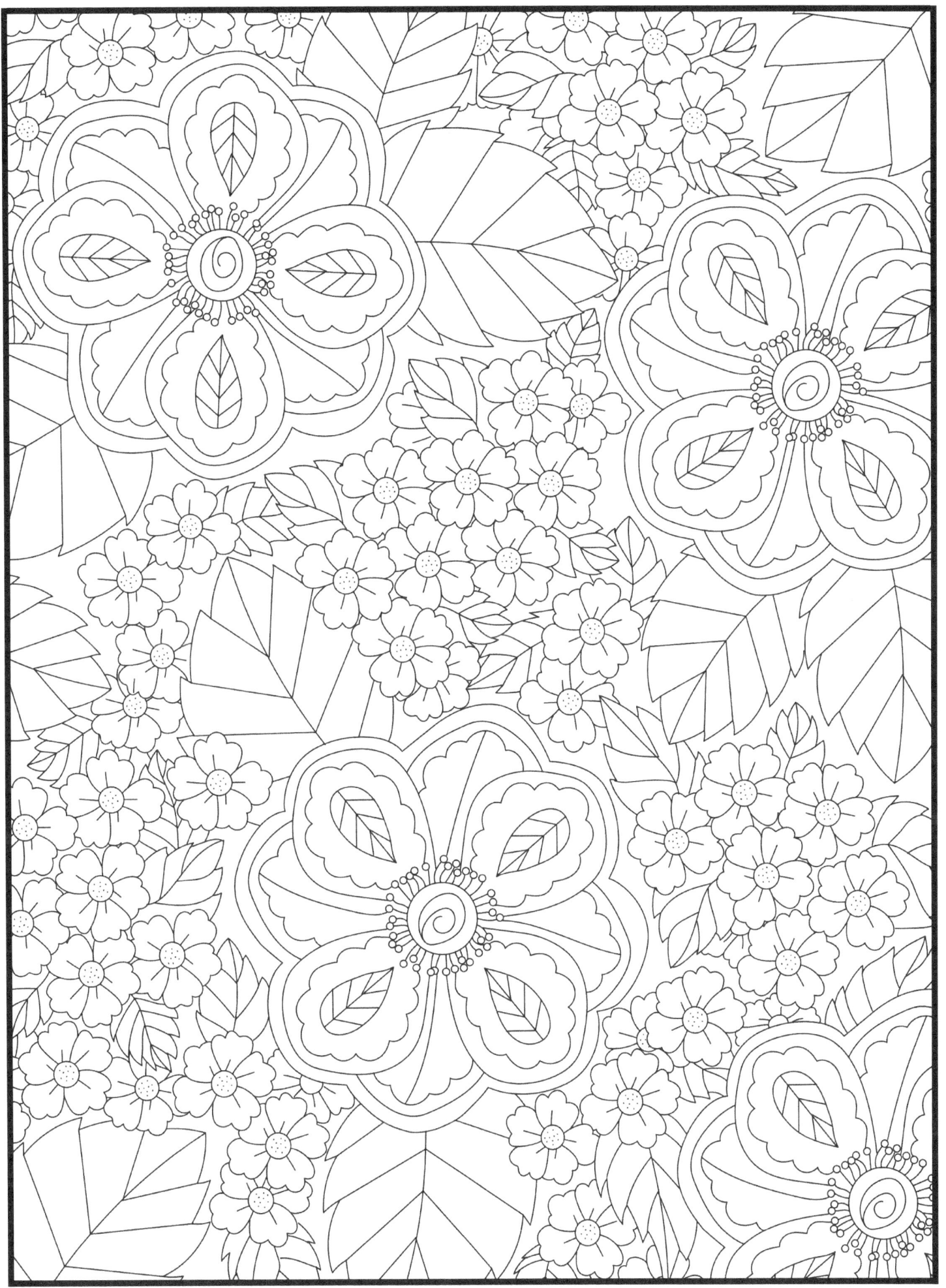

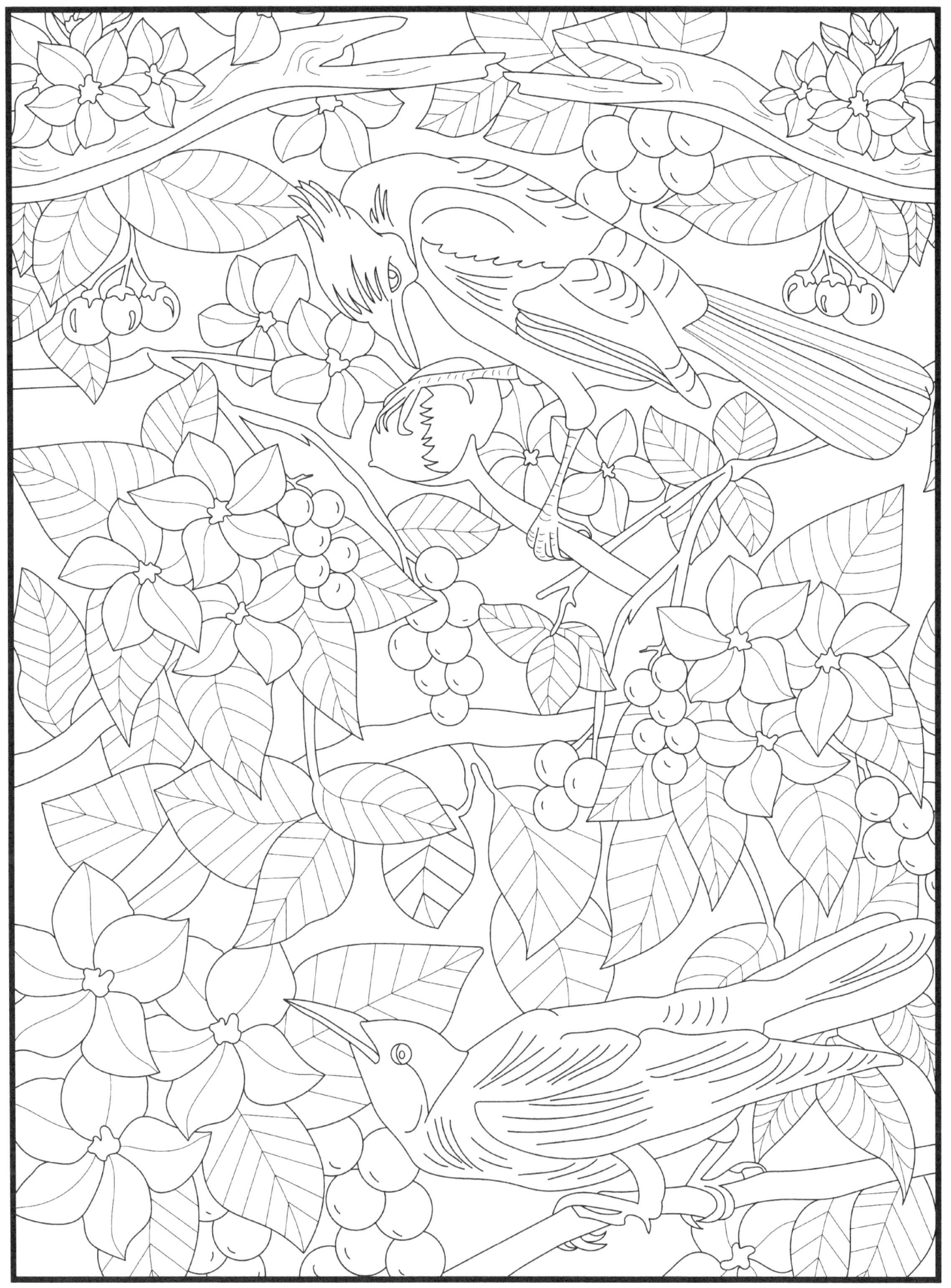

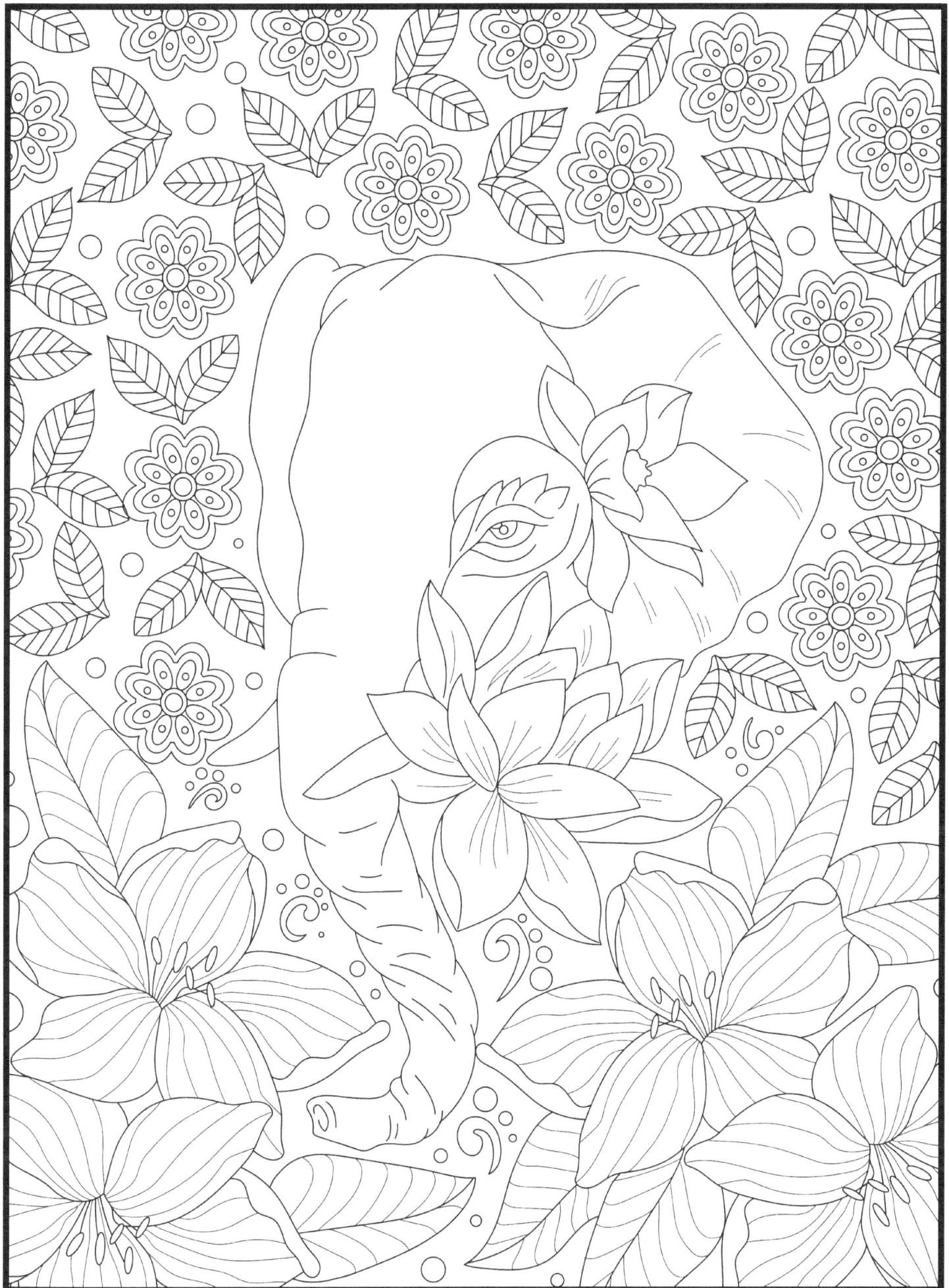

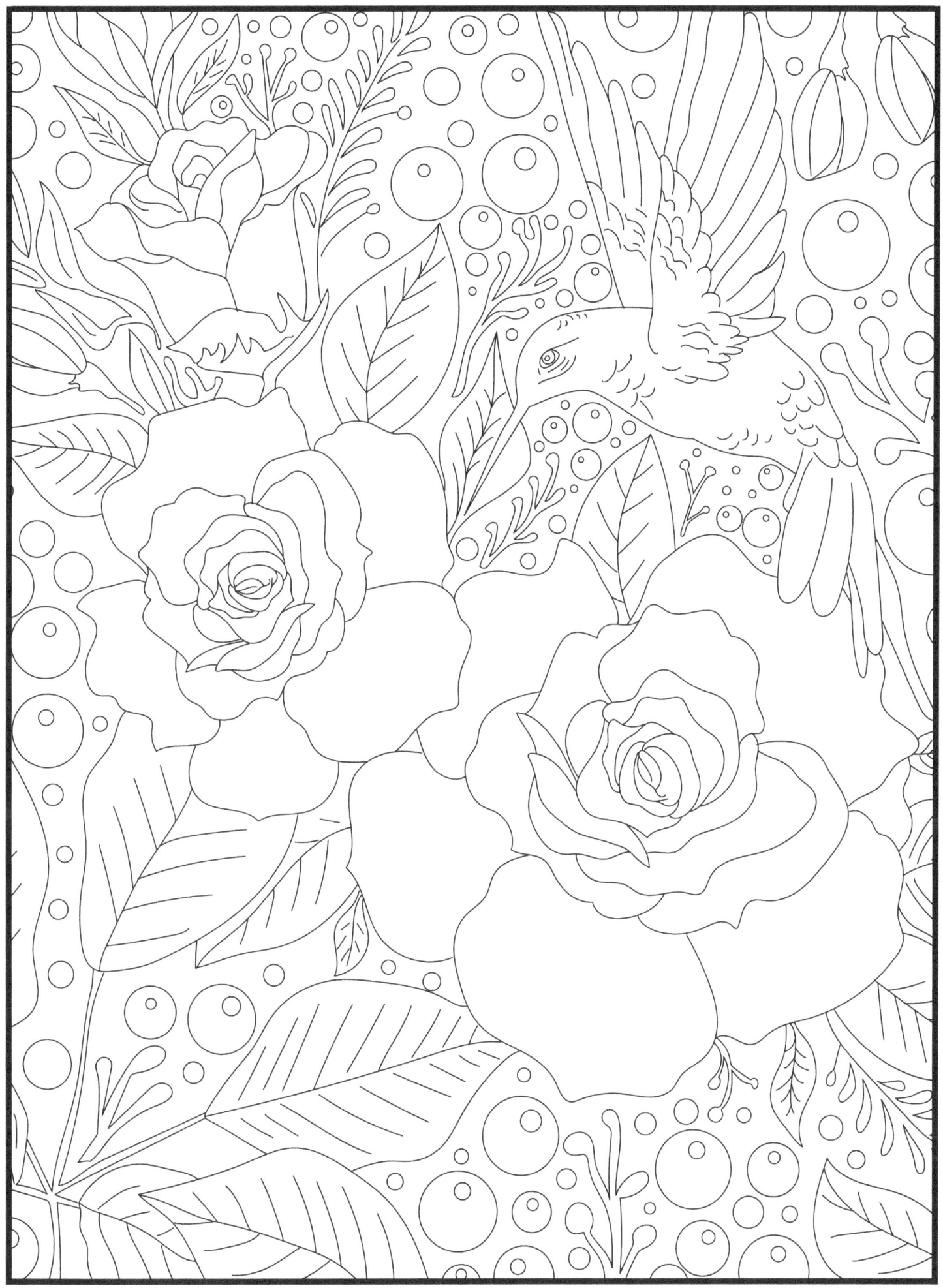

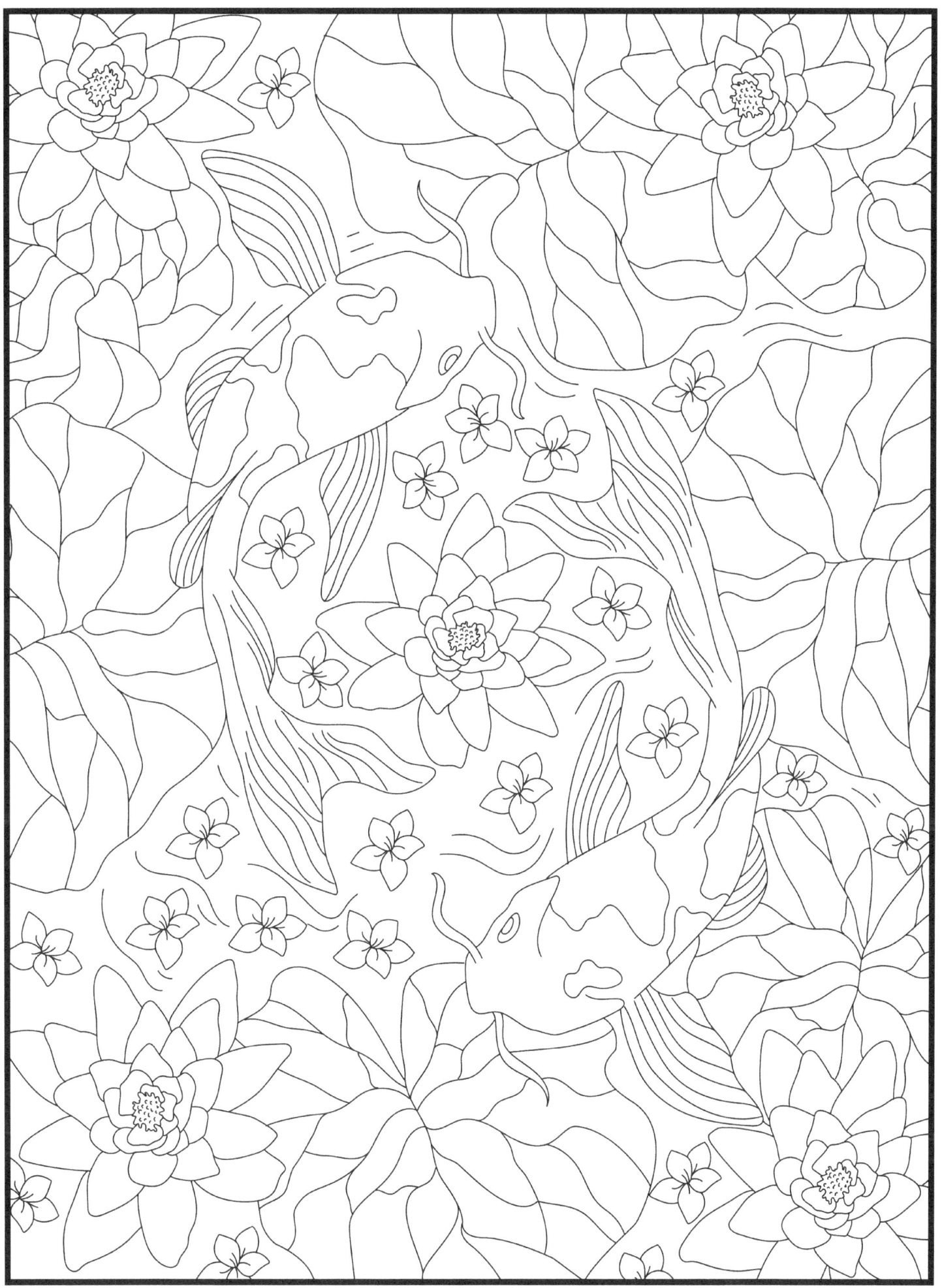

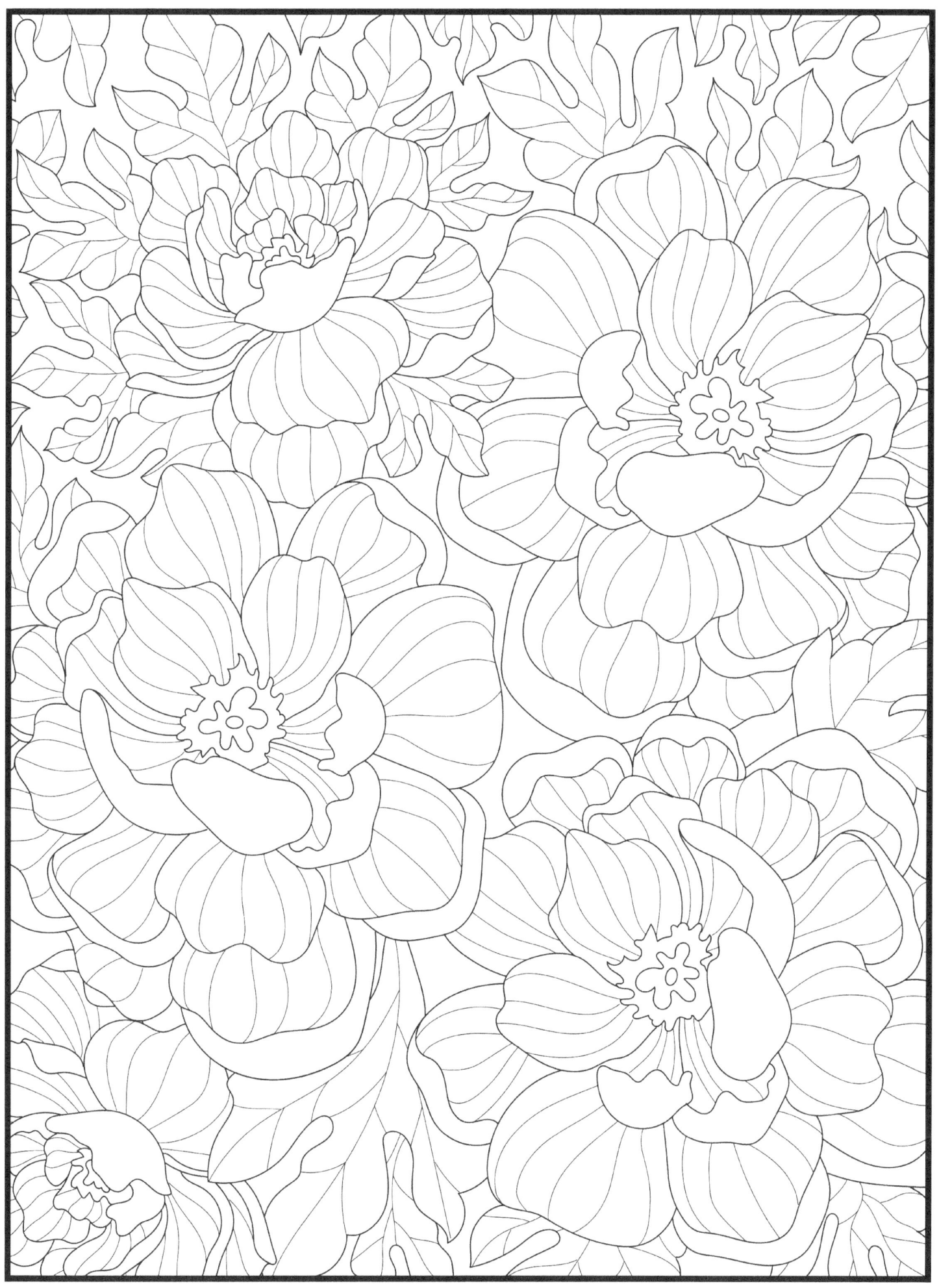

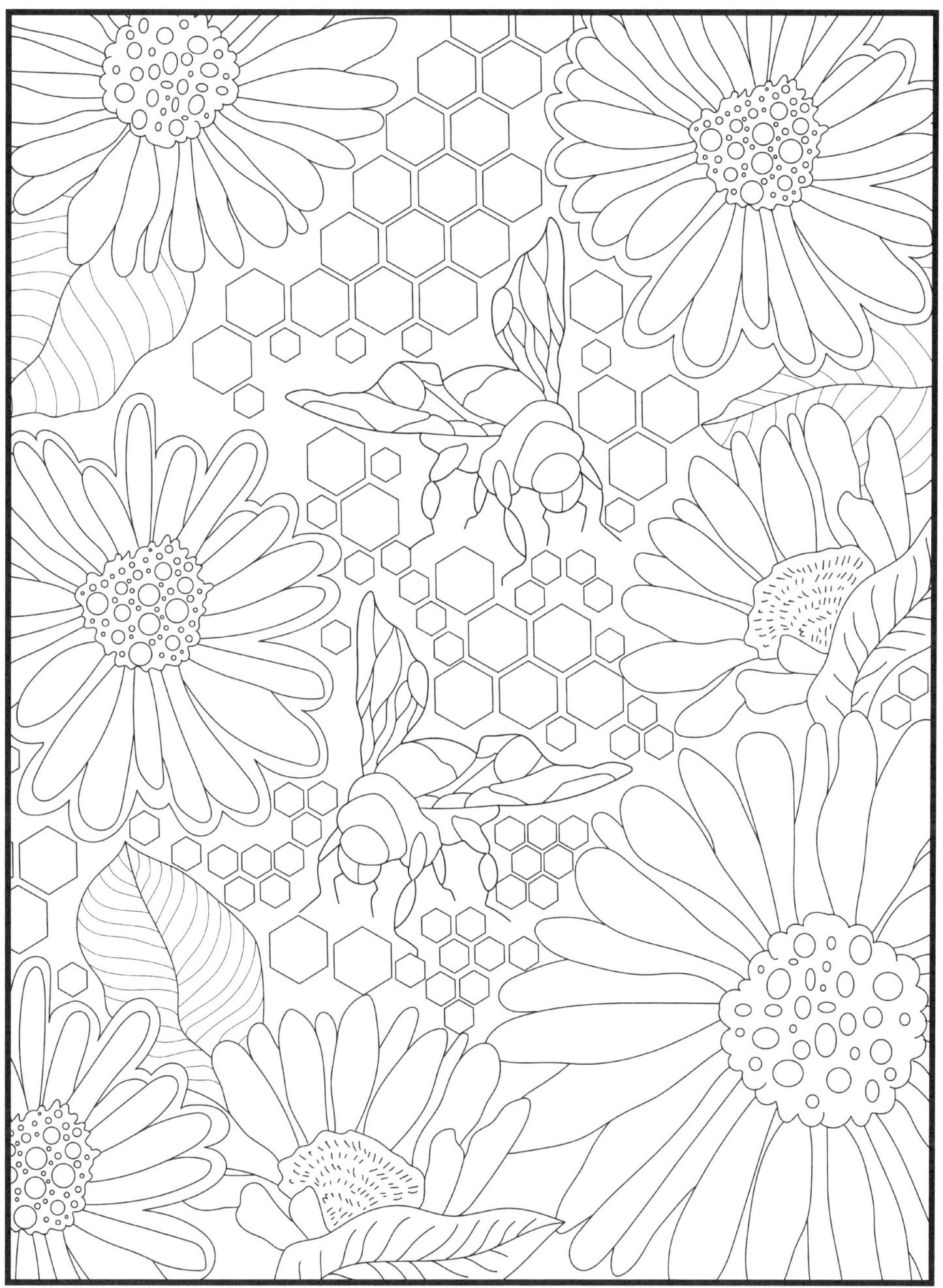

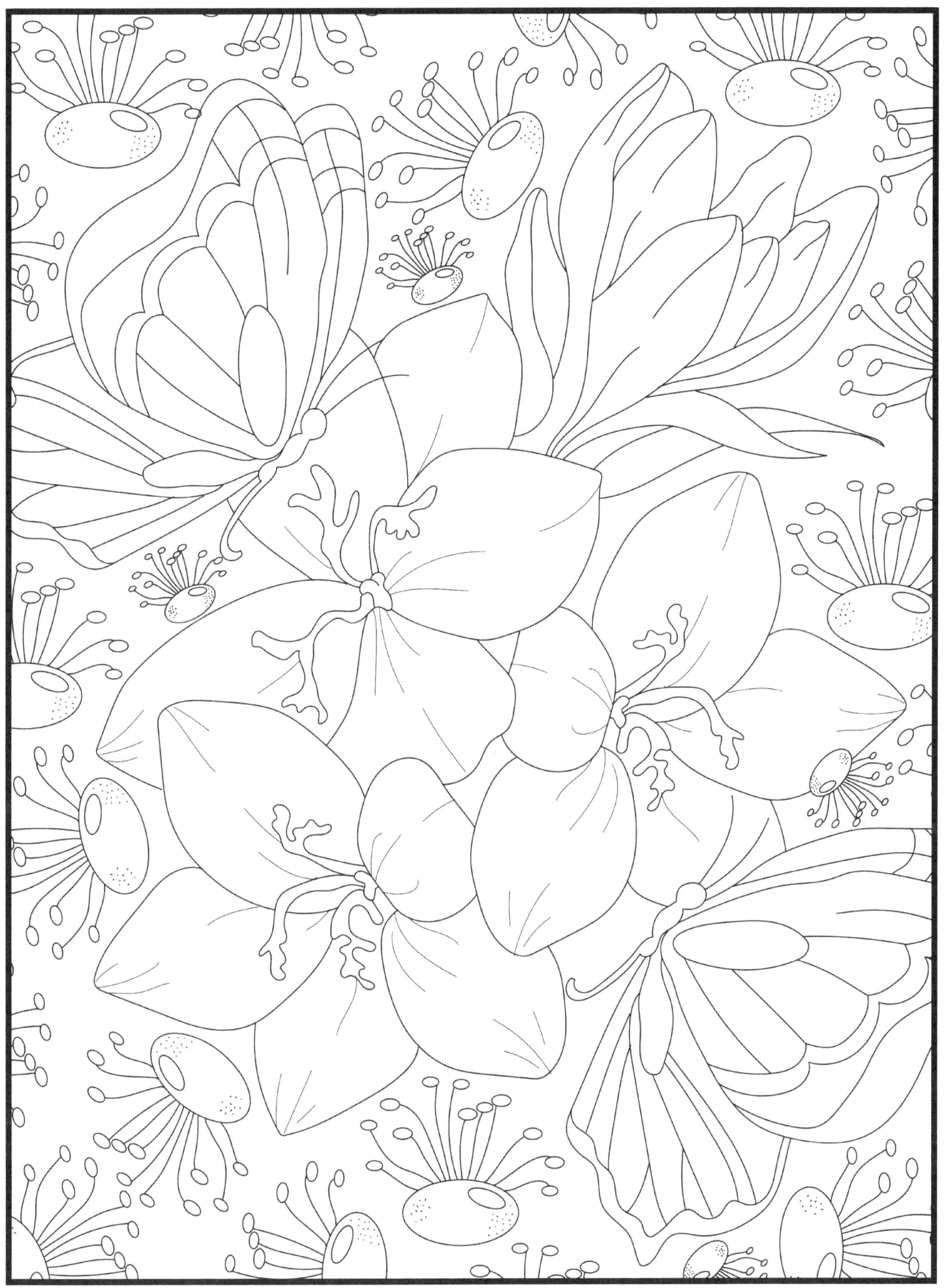

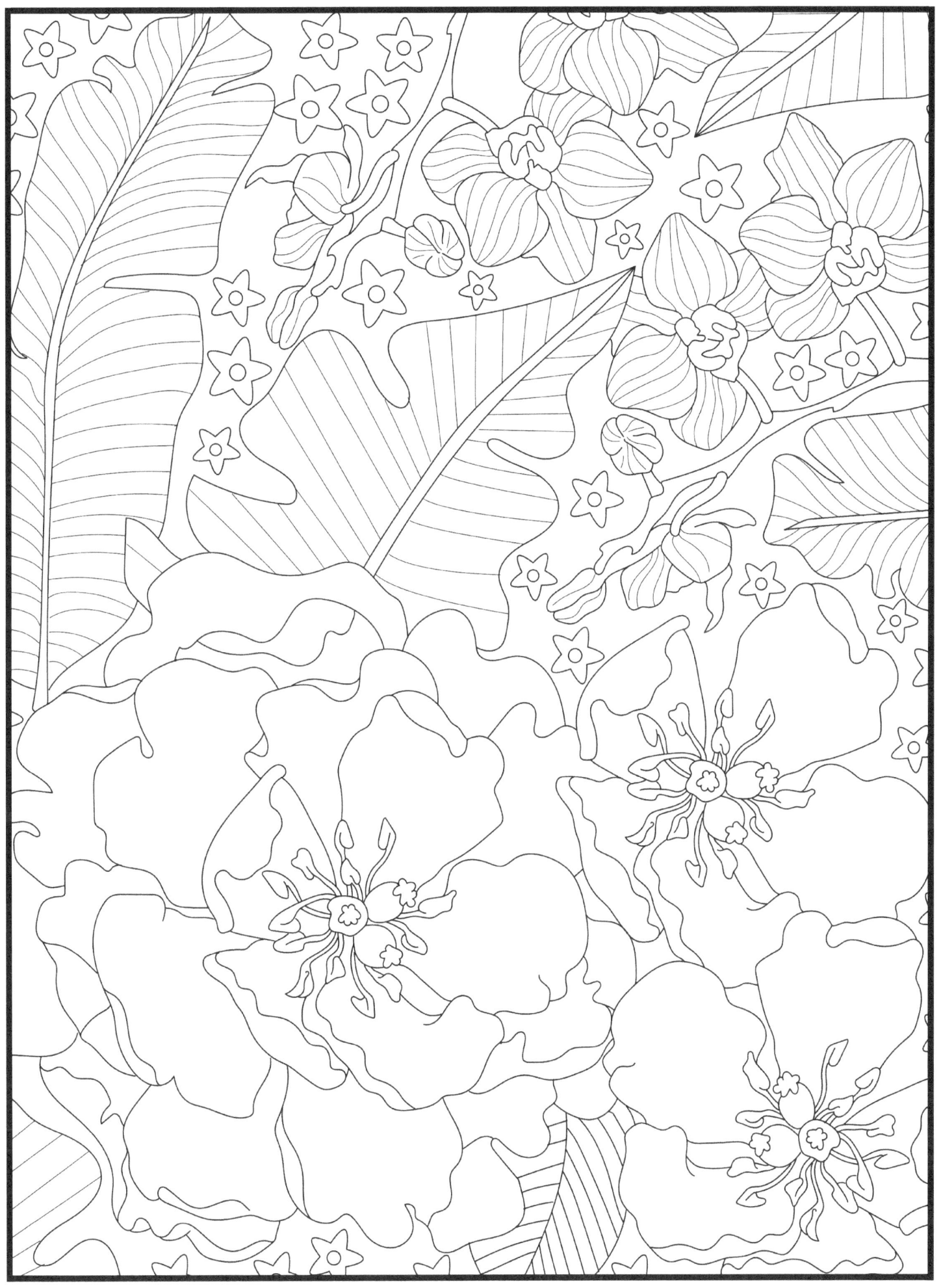

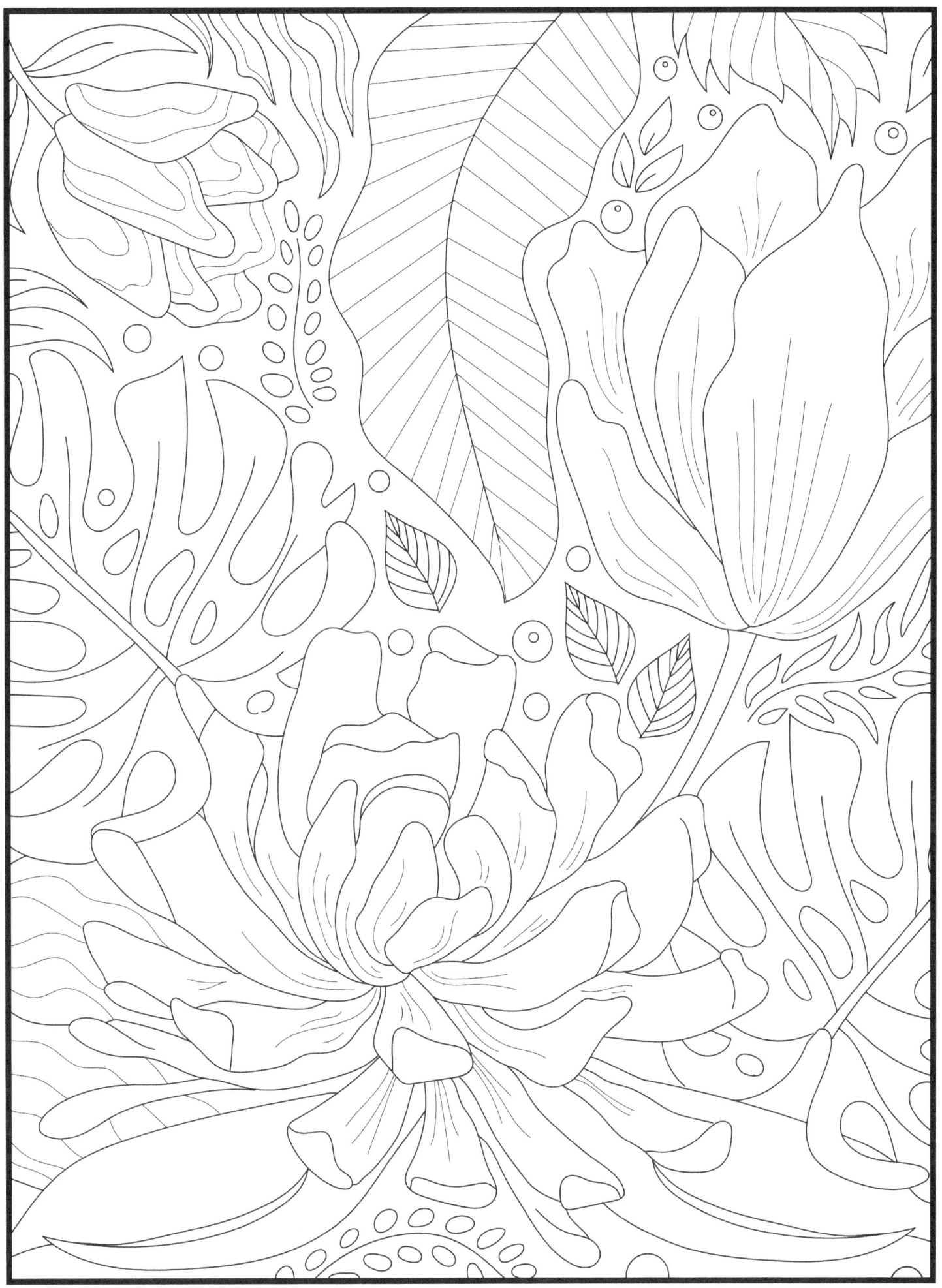

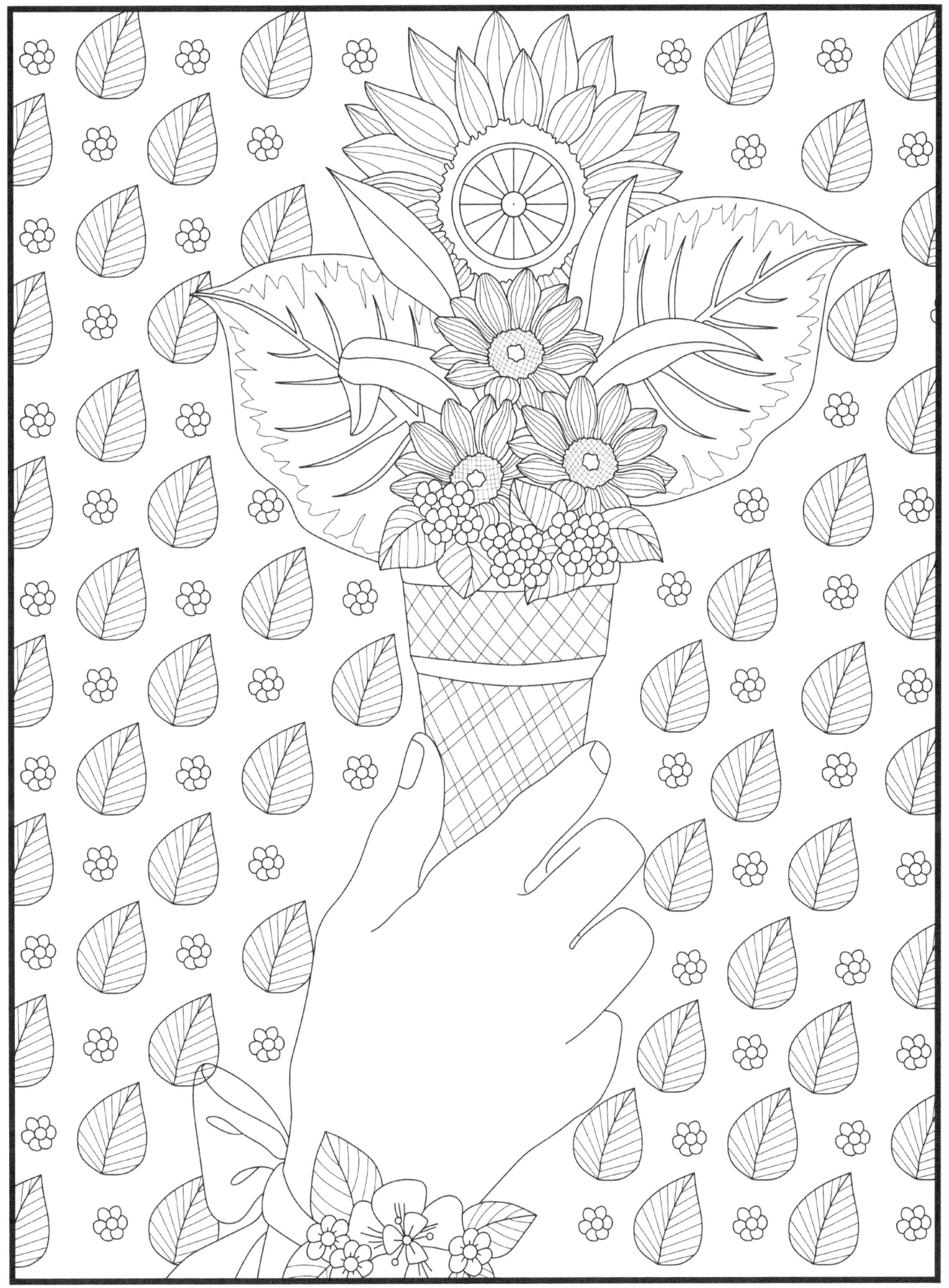

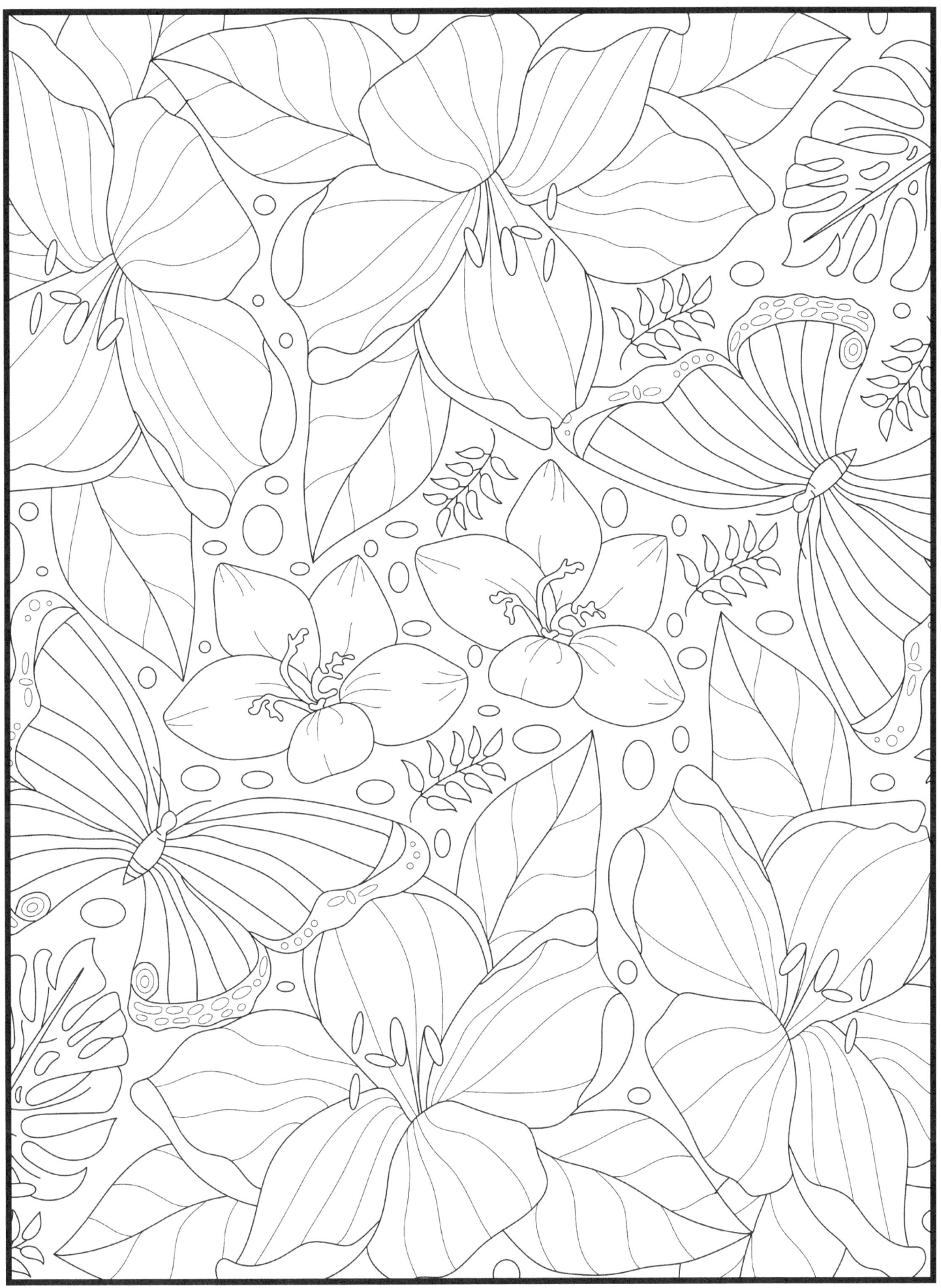

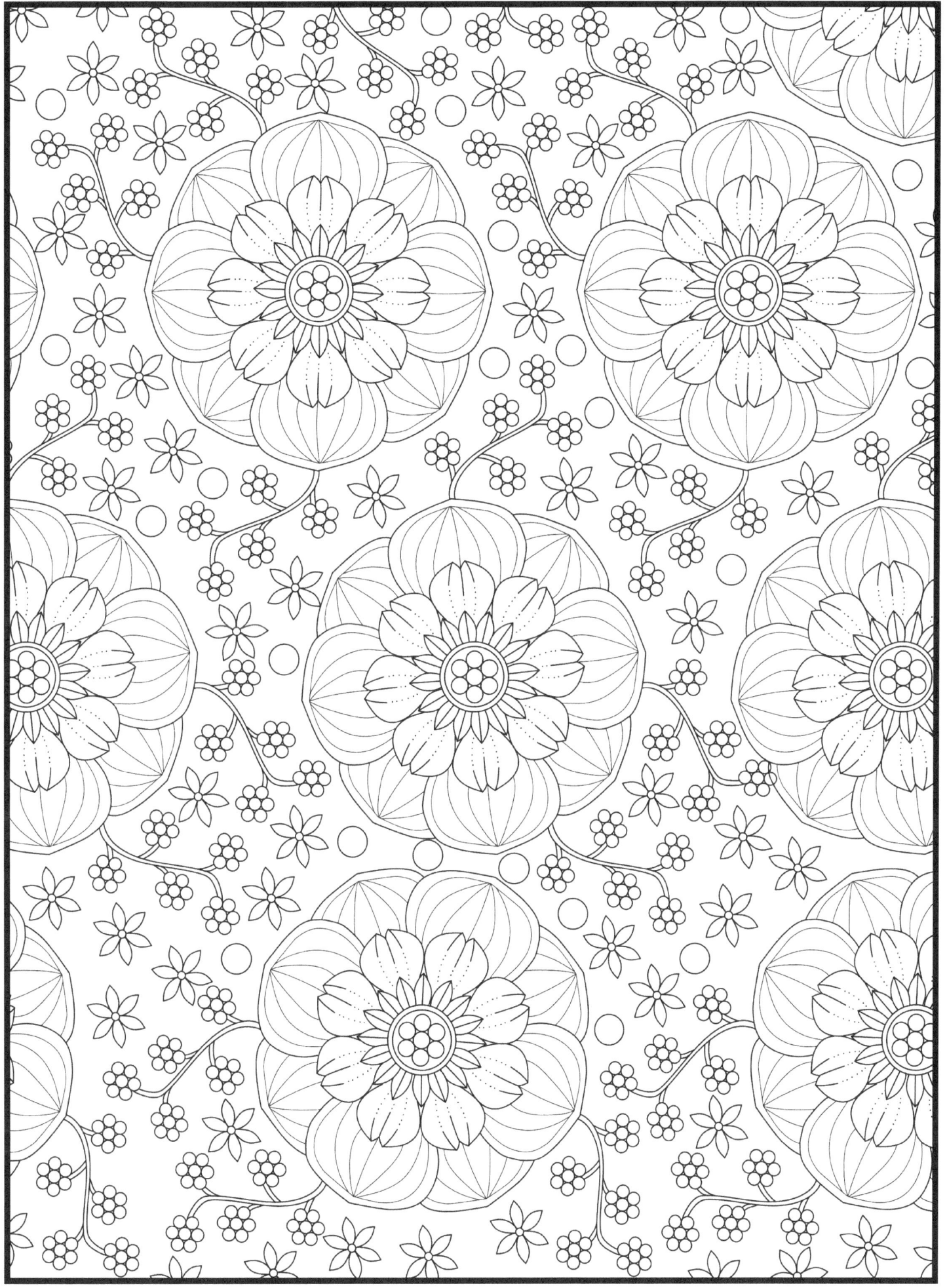

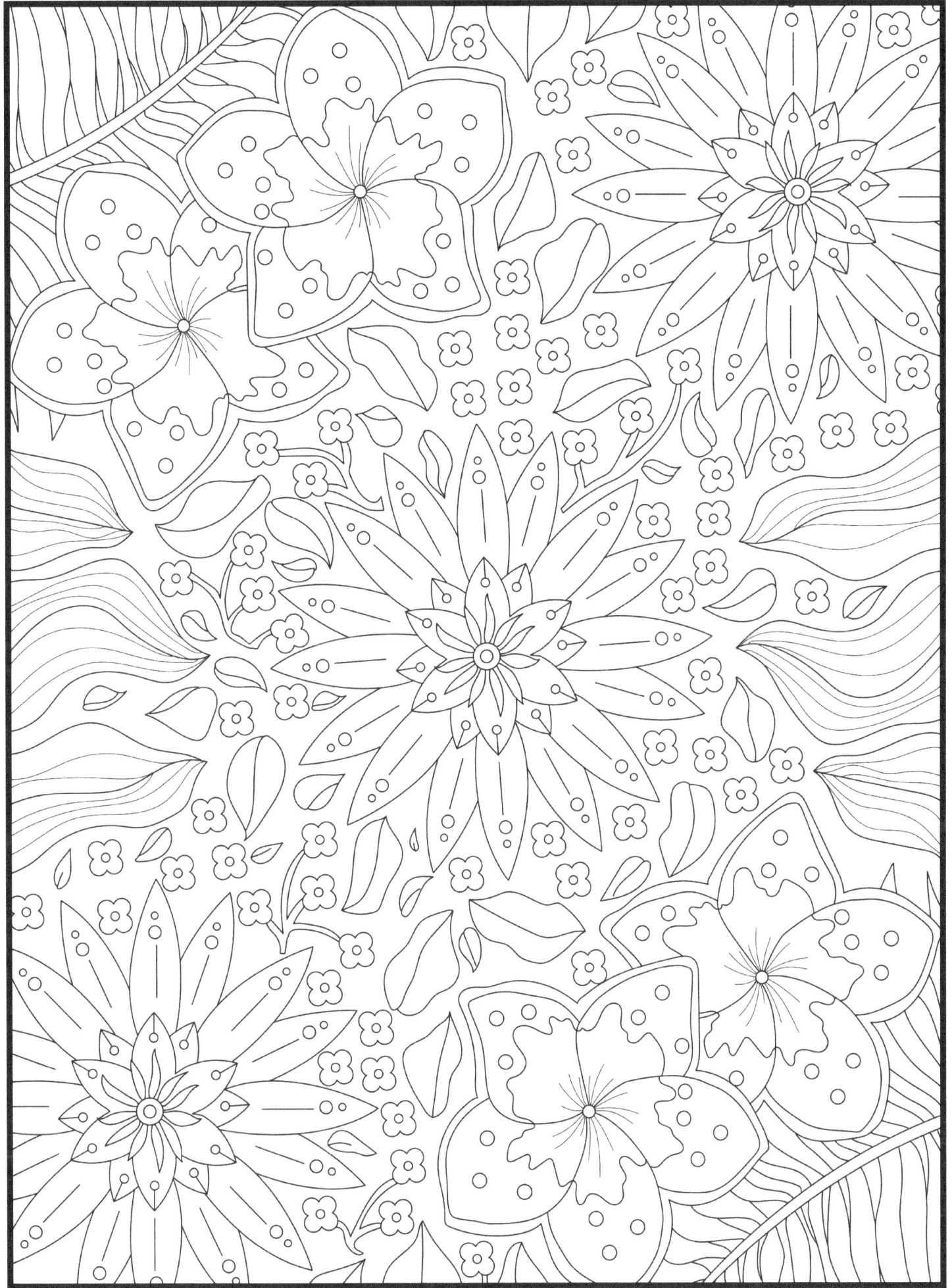

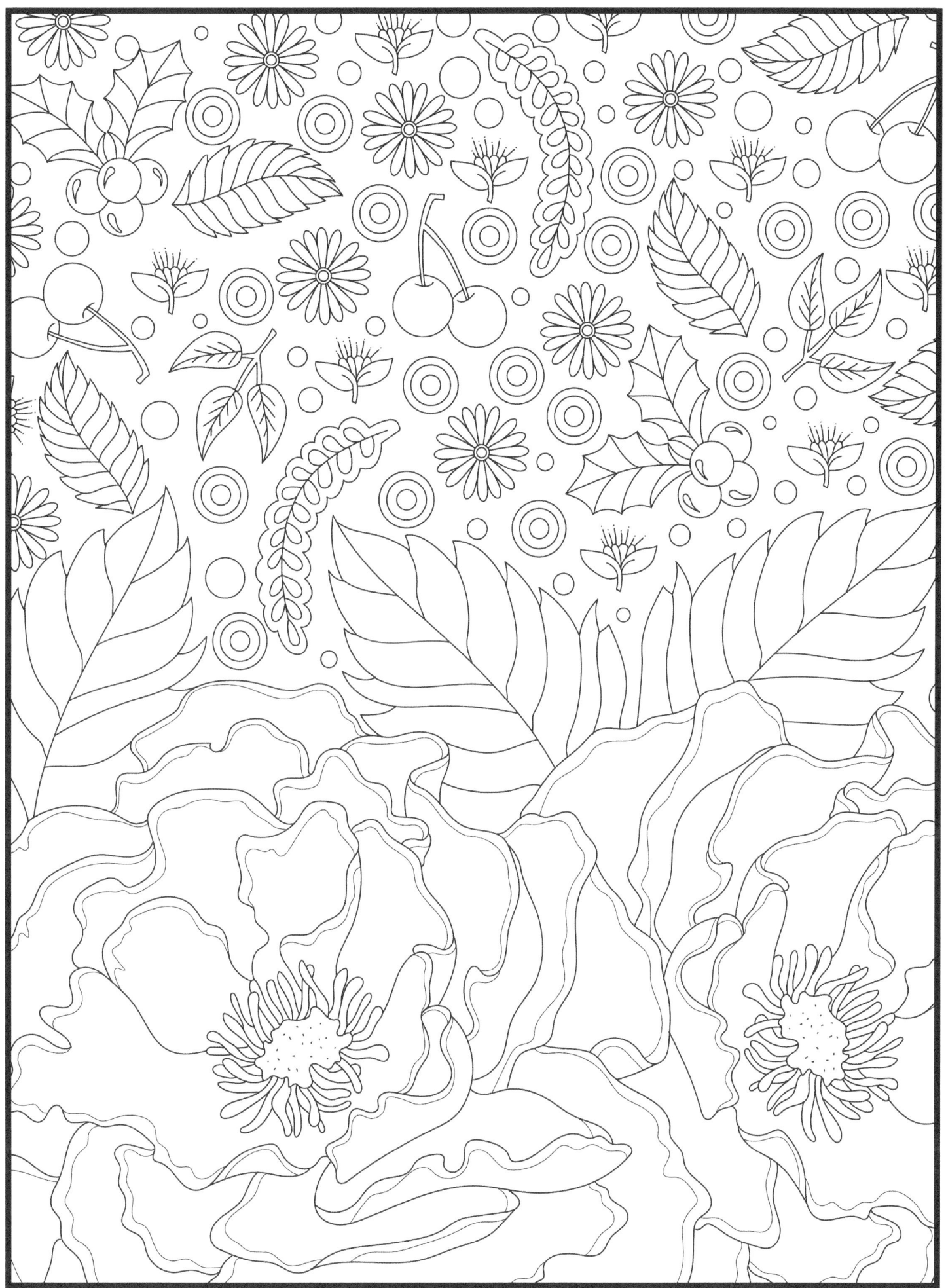

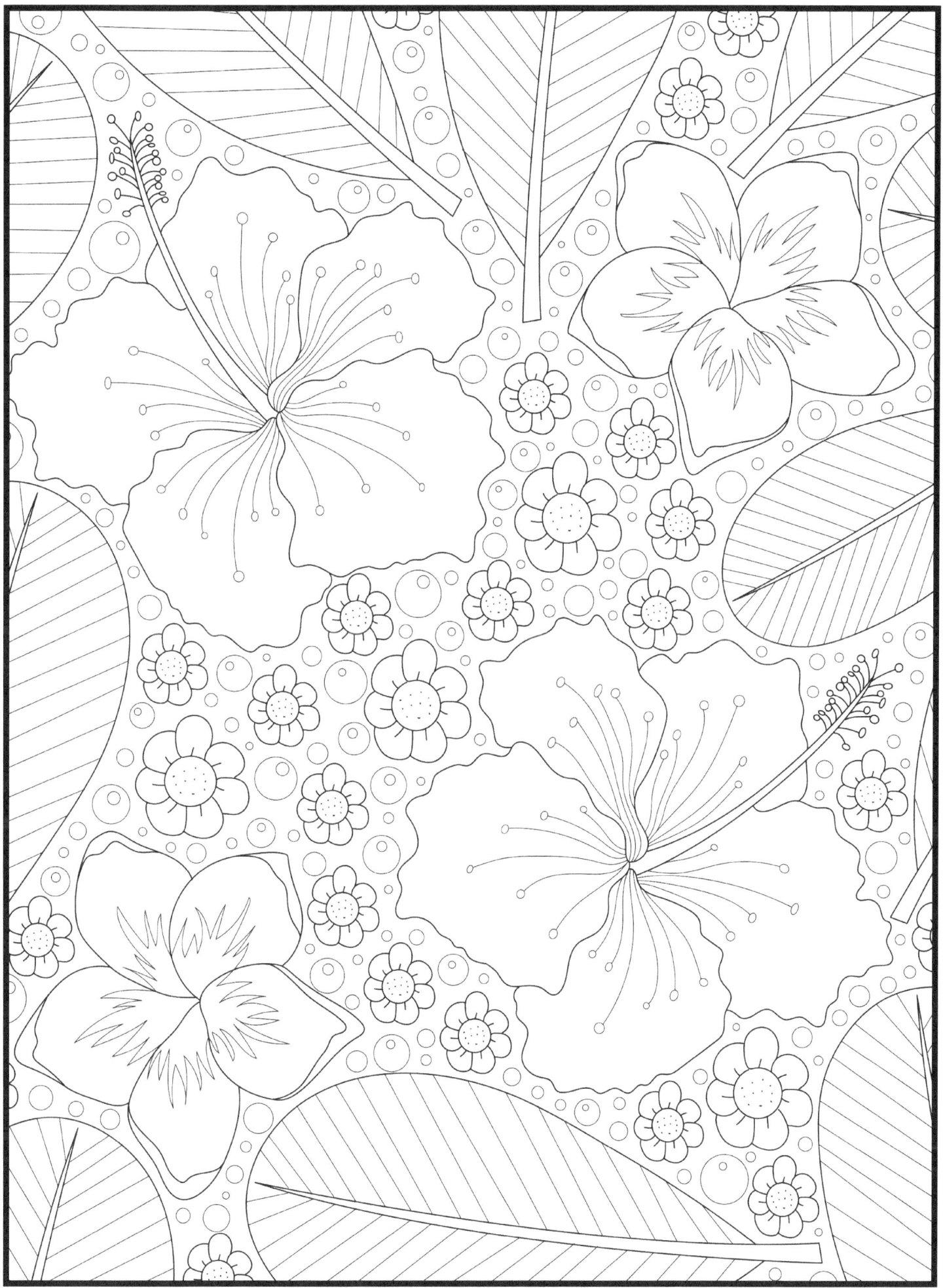

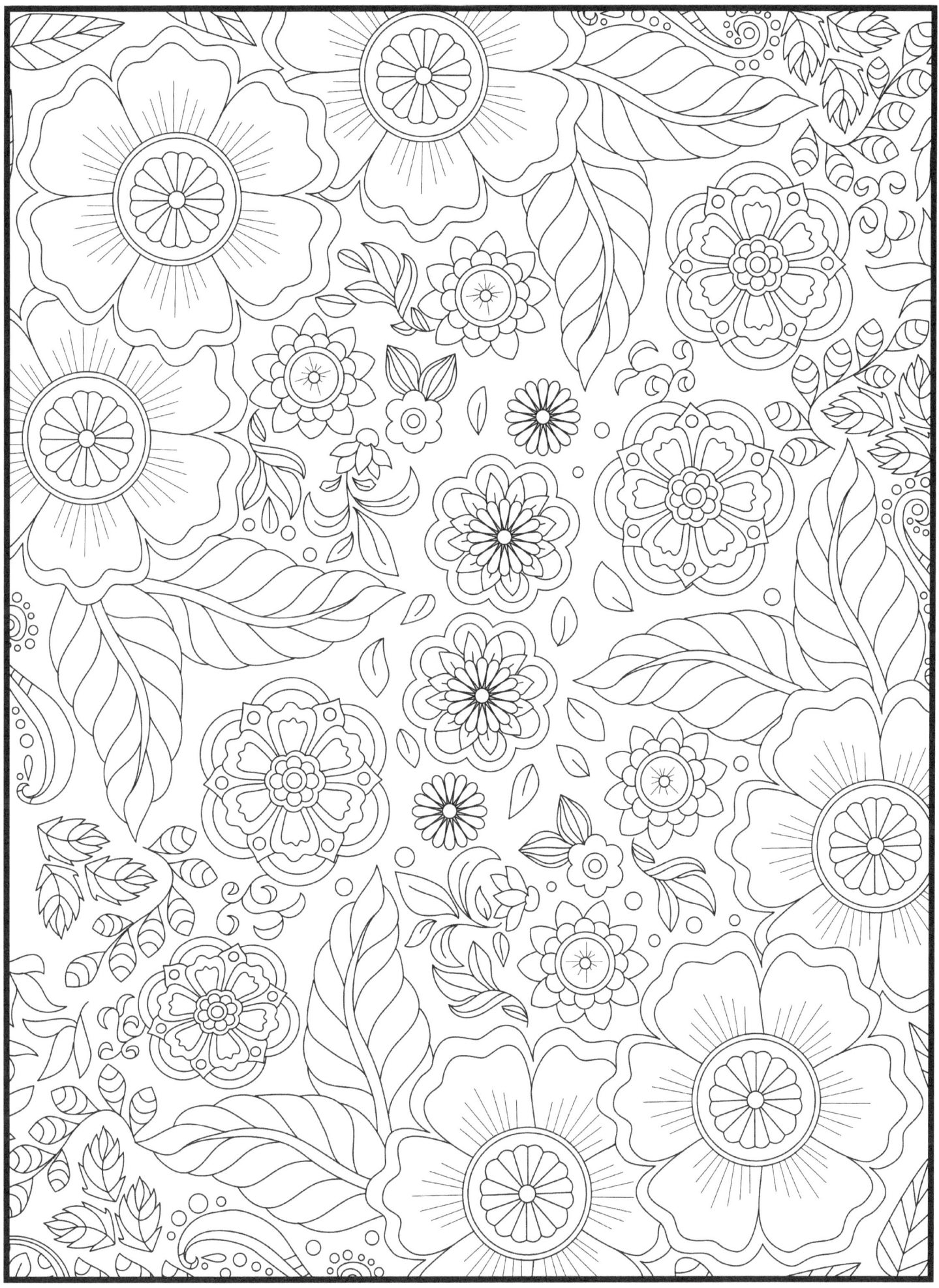

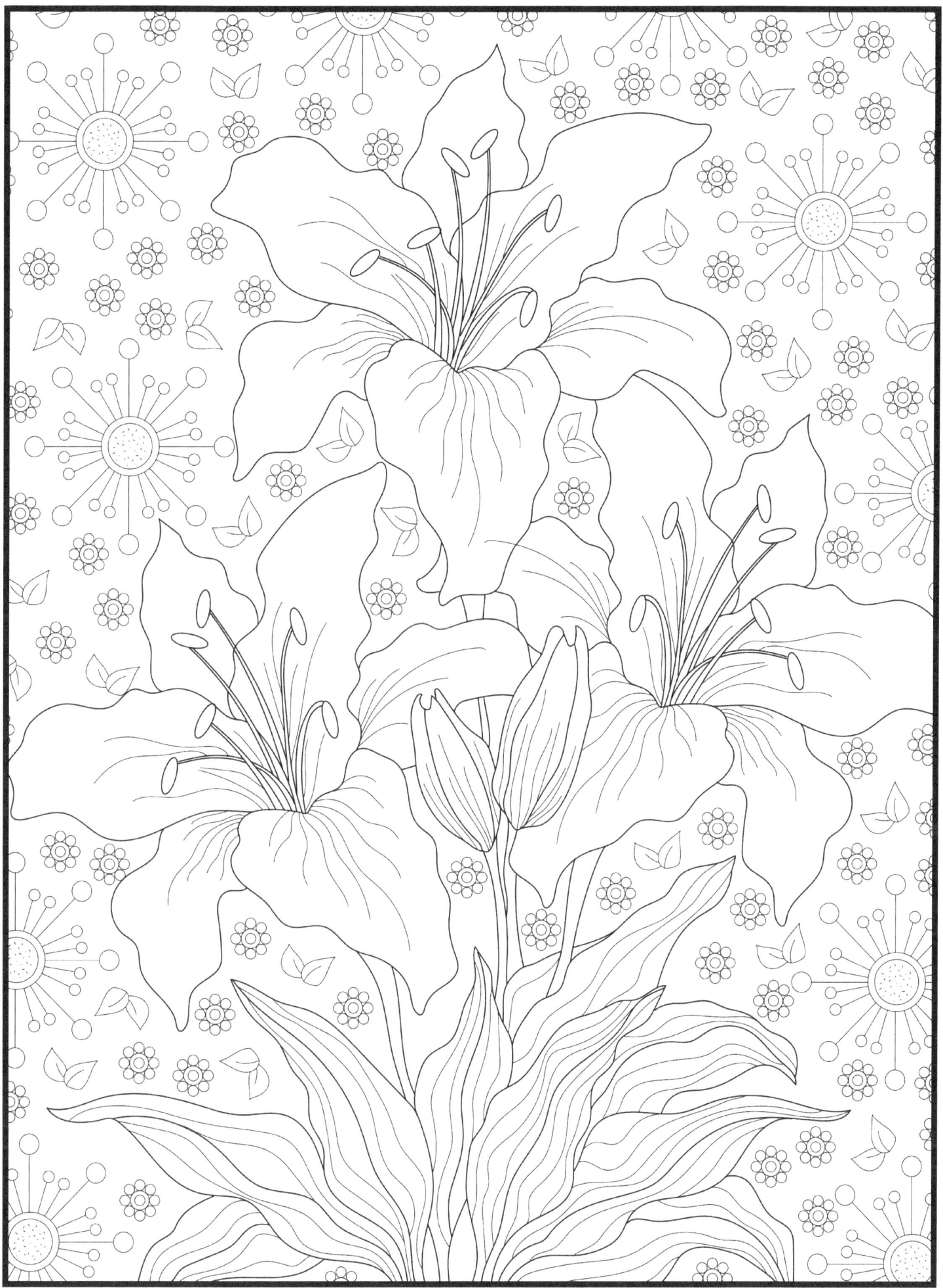

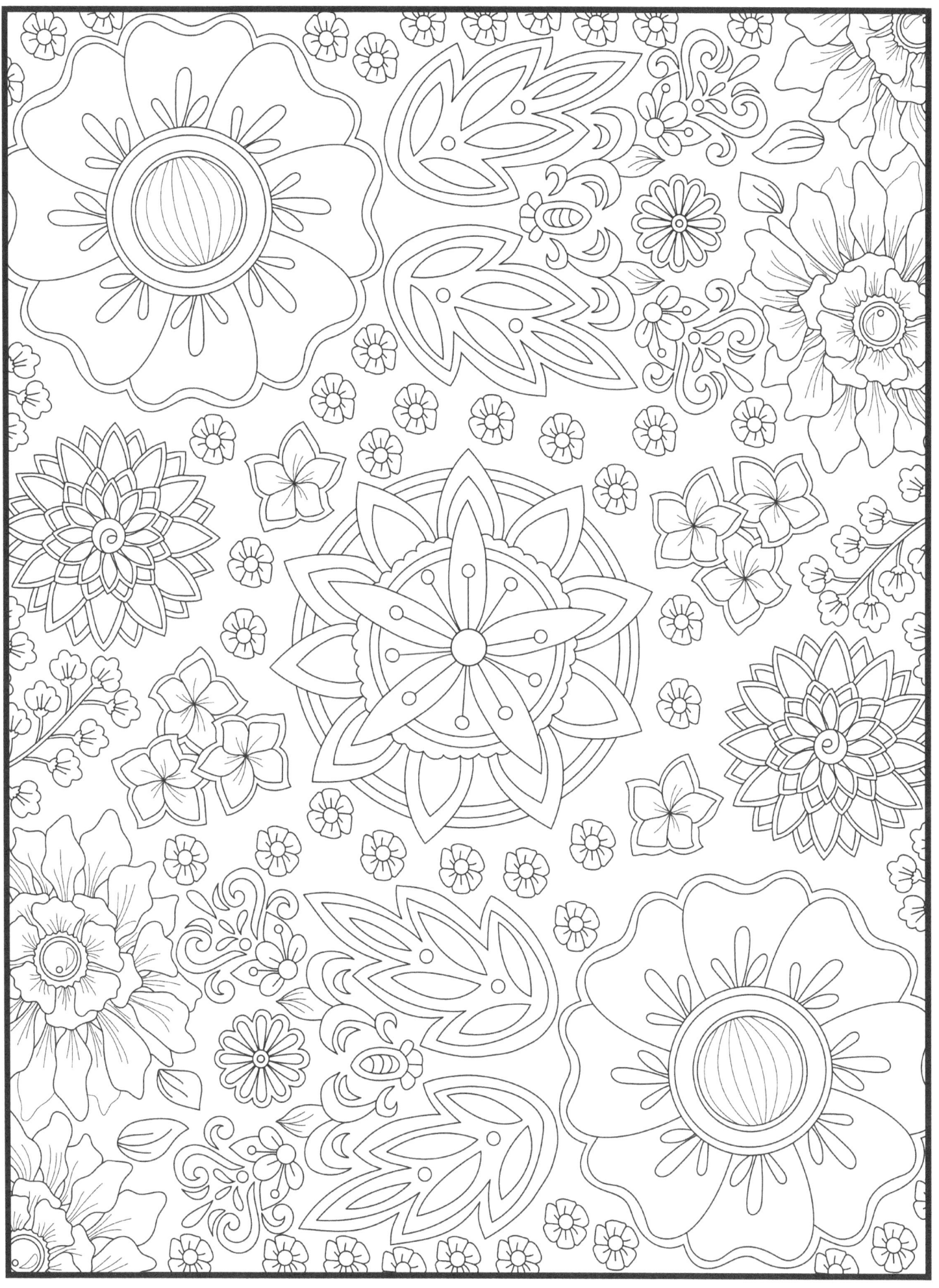

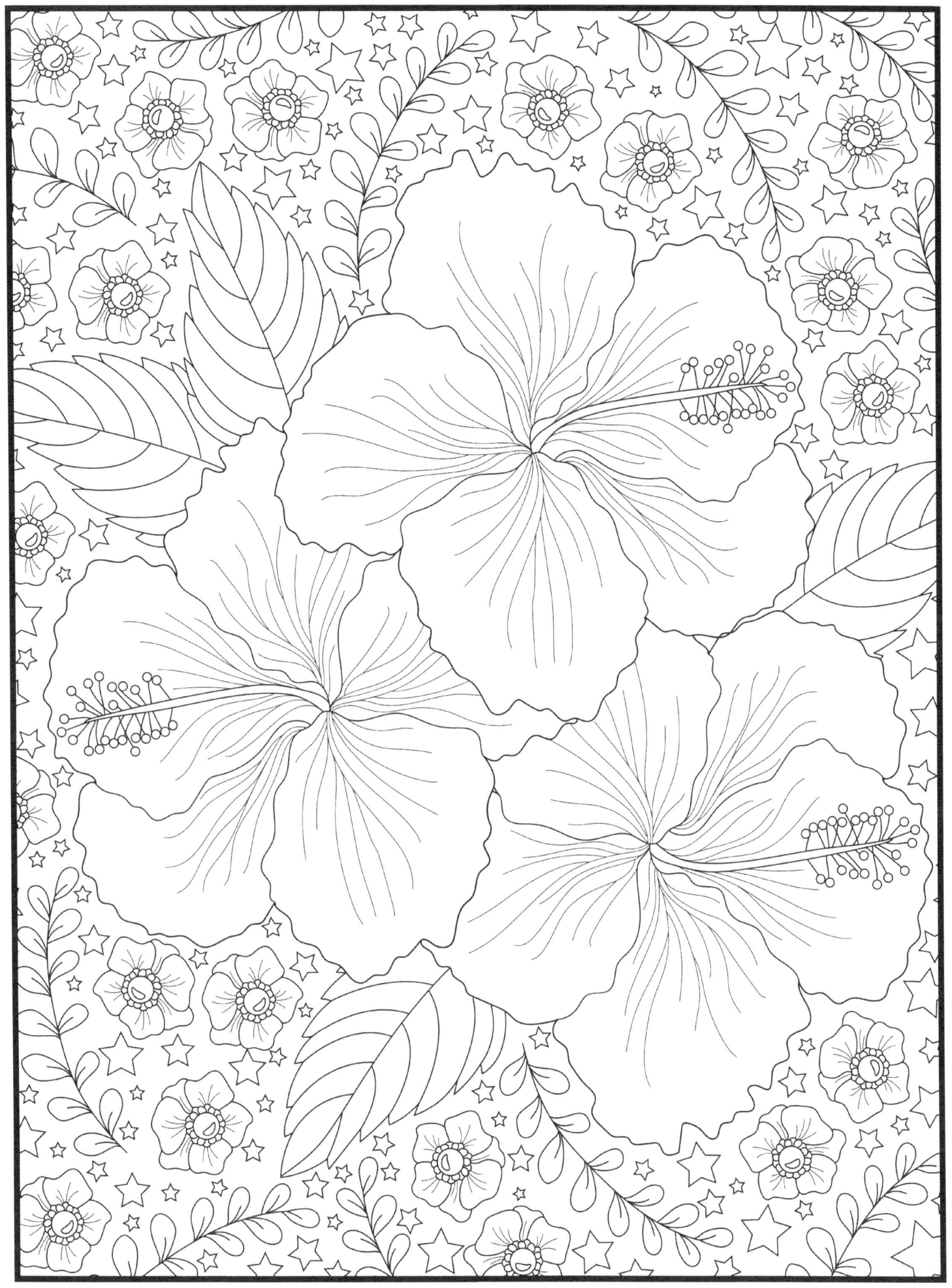

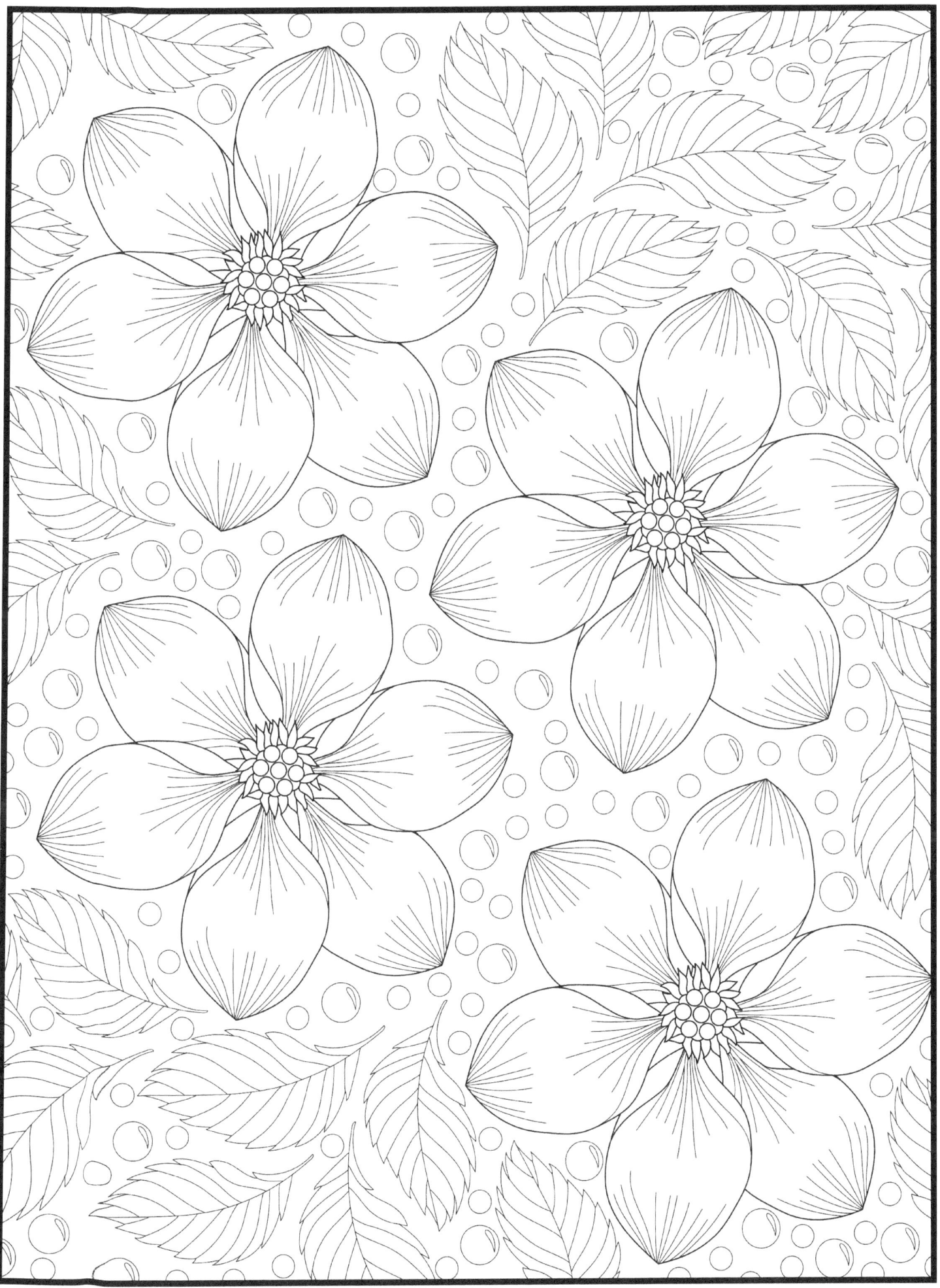

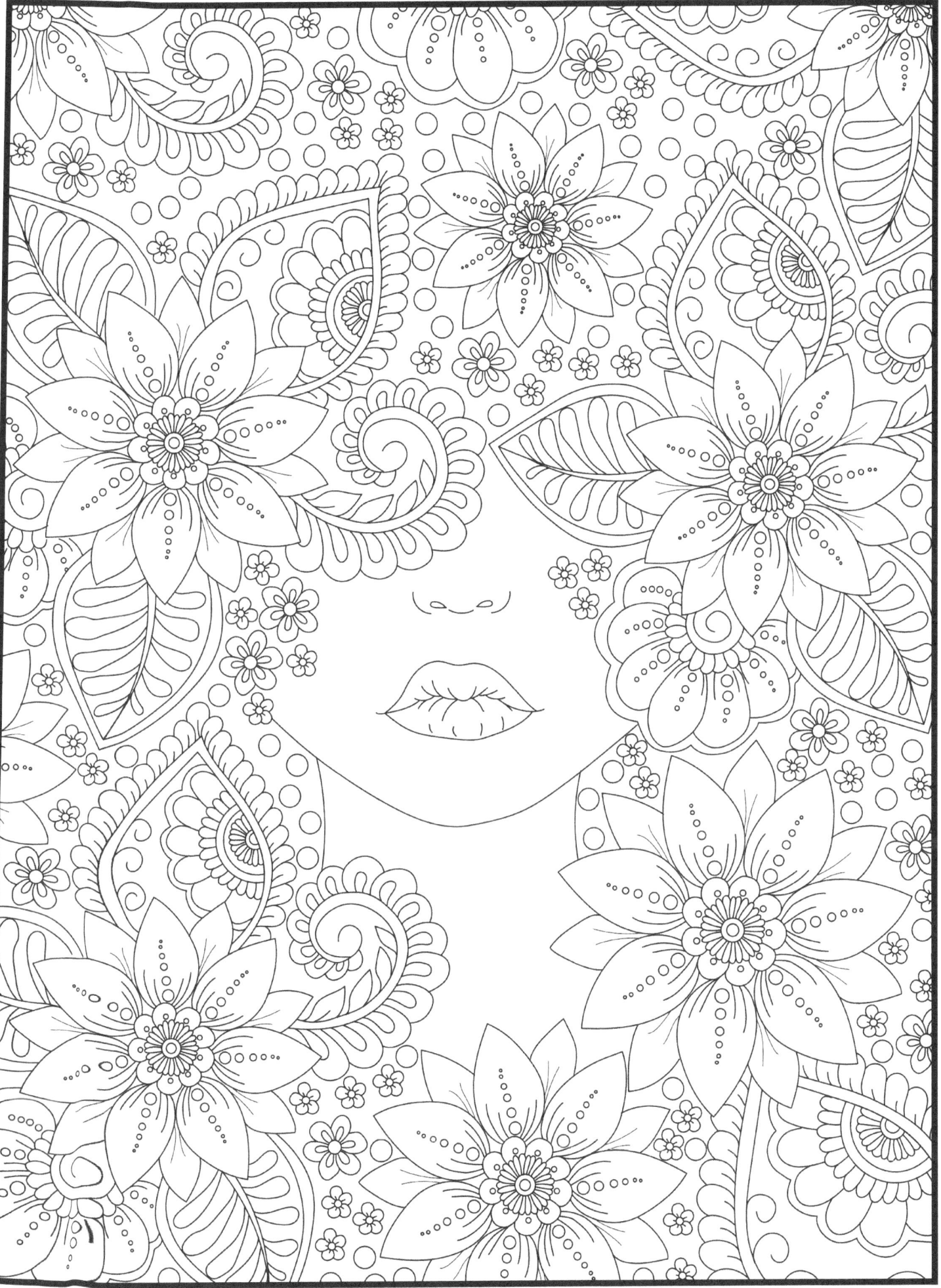

www.ingramcontent.com/pod-product compliance
Lightning Source LLC
Chambersburg PA
CBHW080507220526
45465CB00006B/2407